EVIL MASTERS
The Frightening World of Tyrants

EVIL MASTERS
The Frightening World of Tyrants

Laura Scandiffio

Annick Press Ltd.
Toronto - New York - Vancouver

We acknowledge the support of the Canada Council for the Arts, the Ontario Arts Council, and the Government of Canada through the Book Publishing Industry Development Program (BPIDP) for our publishing activities.

Cataloging in Publication

Scandiffio, Laura
Evil masters : the frightening world of tyrants / written by Laura Scandiffio.

Includes bibliographical references and index.
ISBN 1-55037-895-3 (bound).—ISBN 1-55037-894-5 (pbk.)

1. Dictators—Biography—Juvenile literature.
2. Despotism—History—Juvenile literature. I. Title.

D107.S23 2005   j920.02   C2004-907245-5

The text was typeset in New Baskerville.

Distributed in Canada by:
Firefly Books Ltd.
66 Leek Crescent
Richmond Hill, ON
L4B 1H1

Published in the U.S.A. by
Annick Press (U.S.) Ltd.
Distributed in the U.S.A. by:
Firefly Books (U.S.) Inc.
P.O. Box 1338
Ellicott Station
Buffalo, NY 14205

Printed in China.

Visit us at: www.annickpress.com

To Claire and Gregory
—L.S.

CONTENTS

ACKNOWLEDGMENTS:
Sincere thanks to everyone at Annick Press who helped create this book, especially Rick Wilks, Sheryl Shapiro for her effective design, Sandra Booth for her energetic photo research, and Heather Davies for working on the maps. Thanks also to Barbara Pulling and John Sweet for editing and proofreading the manuscript.
—L.S.

WAYS OF THE TYRANT

Have you ever imagined what it would be like if everyone had to do what you said? What would you do with that kind of power? You might change some things you'd always thought were unfair, or try to turn a dream into reality. Most of us would like to think we would use our power for good.

Nearly all men can stand adversity, but if you want to test a man's character, give him power.
—Abraham Lincoln

But what if the opposite were true—what if you had to obey someone else's every order, every whim? What if that person had no concern for you, or for fairness, and nothing could stop him or her? You would be helpless, at the mercy of a ruler with absolute power. You would be living under a tyrant.

The ancient Greeks were the first to use the word *tyrant* to describe a new kind of leader. These rulers were men who first won the support of the people, then overthrew the government and grabbed power for themselves. Sometimes they passed on their authority to a son. At first the name did not necessarily describe someone evil; that came later. As history was to prove, few people remain pure with so much power in their hands. The English historian Lord Acton famously said, "All power tends to corrupt, and absolute power corrupts absolutely."

Absolute rulers have appeared in many forms since then: kings, queens, and emperors; commanders, popular leaders, and dictators. Whatever his title, each can be described in much the same way: a leader with total control, who uses his power without regard to individual rights and backs up his rule with a military force loyal to him. Though he may claim to act in the name of the people, he is ready to sacrifice them to keep or increase his own power, and he crushes any opposition with force. And while there have been women rulers with tremendous power—queens, empresses, or regents who ruled on behalf of their sons—almost all of history's true tyrants have been men.

Some tyrants accomplish amazing things: they build magnificent architecture or unite a divided, violent society. But they do it at the cost of vast human suffering. They are often people who believe the ends justify any means.

The idea of an absolute monarch who controlled the lives of his subjects probably reached its peak with France's Louis XIV, who summed up how he felt about sharing any power: *"L'état, c'est moi"*—"I *am* the state." Revolutions overthrew many absolute monarchies in Europe and around the world, and people tried to replace them with various kinds of democracy. But in some cases the transition was painful. Crises such as war, poverty, and unemployment troubled the new democracies. Some people, impatient with the arguing and delays that kept the new governments from dealing with urgent problems, longed for a strong leader who could get things done. This rocky start sometimes paved the way for a new and dreadful kind of ruler: the dictators of the twentieth century.

There have been outstanding leaders and poor

ones, and many flawed leaders who did both good and harm while they were in charge. But the tyrant is one who abuses his power to a point that leaves no doubt: his regime is evil.

What are the signs of a tyrant? Can evil leaders be spotted? Tyrants may have ruled in radically different times and places, but they have much in common. The ways they use and abuse power are strikingly similar. It is a pattern that has repeated itself again and again through history.

• **Tyrants usually come to power at a time of turmoil and change.** In fact, they thrive on crisis; it is their route to power. And for a would-be tyrant already in a powerful position, a crisis offers the chance to crush rivals and gather all the reins to himself. Seizing the opportunity presented by a public emergency—such as war, a disaster, or riots—he promises a solution. A strong hand is what's needed to solve the problem, he argues. Often he offers people a scapegoat to blame and fear. The German dictator Adolf Hitler is a prime example. To a defeated nation in the depths of the Depression, he offered himself as a savior. All the country had to do was surrender control to him.

People flock to support the tyrant, expecting the crisis to pass. But it doesn't. His power achieved, the tyrant keeps the nation in a continuous state of emergency. The French revolutionary leader Maximilien Robespierre was accused of refusing to end the revolution. "The conquest of power is a never-ending process," Hitler said, and the Soviet dictator Joseph Stalin also knew the value of making the revolution permanent. In the tyrant's scheme, the whole of society is kept striving towards a goal that is always just out of reach: another five-year plan for the economy, a more complete purge of traitors, mobilizing for war. The First Emperor of Qin kept his subjects toiling on one gigantic building scheme after another. People striving desperately to reach a goal don't have the energy or the time for rebellion. And without the sense of crisis, it might become obvious how purposeless and terrible the tyrant's regime is.

• **Tyrants are masters of propaganda—campaigns to manipulate the opinions and emotions of a population.** The goal is to influence the attitudes and beliefs of as many people as possible. Books, newspapers, films, and posters can all be used to broadcast propaganda, as can symbols such as flags and monuments. Long before modern dictators used TV and radio to flood the nation with their views, regimes used other tactics to get their message across. The Qin emperor dotted China with stone inscriptions that told everyone how good life was under his dominion. Whether in speeches or in print, in classrooms or in the mass media, tyrants repeat in many ways the same basic messages: their aims are the only right way to go, and life is better under their rule. Just as important, propaganda creates the illusion that everyone supports the regime.

A key element of this propaganda is the image built up around the leader himself. He is portrayed as larger than life, heroic, wise, never wrong. He often links himself with the most popular religion, making himself its chief figurehead. The cult of personality is sometimes taken to outrageous lengths, making the leader seem like a god on earth.

This has made many people wonder: does the tyrant believe his own propaganda? Surrounded by flattery and symbols of their power, some rulers may start to believe the myth they helped create, and think they really are special and always right. The Qin emperor came to believe what his government told everyone else: he was superhuman and divine. This delusion can be one of the causes of a tyrant's destruction.

• **Propaganda is most effective when there is no one to contradict it.** Once in power, tyrants smother all voices of opposition, especially those of scholars, writers, and others who might analyze the regime and criticize it. Book burning has been a sign of tyranny throughout the ages. Those who piled books onto bonfires might claim they were rejecting old ideas not in keeping with the new revolutionary spirit—throwing out the garbage they didn't want in the new world they were building. But destroying knowledge and censoring ideas is a dangerous path to take. The philosopher Heinrich Heine warned, "Those who burn books will in the end burn people." His words were as true for the First Emperor of Qin as they would be for Adolf Hitler—whose party members burned Heine's books, among many others.

Ideas are more dangerous than guns. We wouldn't let our enemies have guns, why would we let them have ideas?
—Stalin

By censoring what people can say and write, and by imprisoning or killing critics, the tyrant takes control of the truth. Like the drum roll that drowned out the last words of victims guillotined by France's revolutionary government, the tyrant's message is clear: Don't speak unless I want you to, and then I will give you the words. Don't think for yourself; I will tell you what to think.

• **Tyrants strive to change the way people think, and they pay special attention to the young generation.** Adults may be set in their ways or remember enough of the past to be skeptical of the current regime, but young people don't have the same long memories or conflicting loyalties. Tyrants see them as blank slates they can imprint with their own ideas.

If the tyrant's power is to endure, a key task is grooming youth to play the role mapped out for them in the new society. Controlling what they learn in school is crucial. Children in Stalin's Russia were instructed to tear pages out of their history textbooks or paste new, state-approved versions overtop. Hitler and Stalin recognized the potential of influencing young Germans and Russians through their peers: millions of young people had their beliefs shaped by the Hitler Youth and its Soviet counterpart, the Young Pioneers. "While the older generation could still waver," Hitler declared confidently, "the younger generation has pledged itself to us and is ours, body and soul."

You must encircle the adults through their sons.
—Saddam Hussein

• **No population can be controlled for long unless the tyrant backs up his orders with another tool—terror.** Violence and the threat of violence, against either groups or random victims, together create a climate where no one feels safe. Who will be next? People compete with each other to look loyal. They lower their eyes, pretending not to see their neighbors being arrested. Maybe they'll be spared if they lie low.

To inspire fear, a tyrant typically recruits an armed force loyal to him personally. The troops may start out as bodyguards, but throughout the reign of terror they grow in number and power. Besides protecting the tyrant and intimidating the population, these special troops are his eyes and ears.

• **Tyrants often show signs of xenophobia—a fear of foreigners and their influence.** Many refuse to travel. Hitler brushed off suggestions that he might explore the world to broaden his horizons, or perhaps learn another language. "What could I learn that's new?" he shrugged. Joseph Stalin was also reluctant to learn about the rest of the world first-hand.

What were they afraid of? Besides the risk of being overthrown while away, seeing another way of life might challenge their fixed ideas, which every tyrant guards against criticism or attack. Isolating their domain from the rest of the world is also important. Foreigners and their ideas must be shut out of the realm because they could sway the minds of the tyrant's subjects. "Our young must be taught to fear and distrust foreigners," said Iraq's Saddam Hussein.

• **The longer he is in power, the more suspicious a tyrant becomes.** He sees enemies everywhere, even among supporters who helped him get where he is. Because he rules through fear, the tyrant builds a trap for himself. He is isolated physically by his guarded walls and squads of special police, but in other ways too. No one dares tell him the truth. Surrounded only by people who flatter him because they're afraid, he is never criticized and so never learns from his mistakes. He also senses that he is constantly being lied to, which makes him more suspicious than ever.

What kind of person becomes a tyrant? What fuels an ambition for absolute power? Some may have been born into a position of power, but why did they abuse that position, and how could they live with their crimes? And what about self-made tyrants—what drives them in the uphill battle to take power, often destroying allies and friends who helped them along the way?

The man who is born to be a dictator is not compelled; he wills it. He is not driven forward, but drives himself.
—Hitler

A closer look at the rulers themselves is revealing. They are alike in many ways, but they have differences too. Some are magnetic personalities with great charisma, while others are surprisingly bland and likely to be underestimated. While Hitler had the gift of drawing massive crowds with his explosive speeches, Stalin was not a captivating person; his specialty was quietly intimidating people in small meetings. But the similarities among tyrants are much more intriguing.

- **Many of them were brutalized in childhood.** Some—like Hitler, Stalin, and Saddam—were abused as children. Others, like Ivan the Terrible or the emperor Nero, witnessed acts of cruelty at a tender age or, like Robespierre, were torn from those they loved. They were left feeling deeply insecure in a world they saw as cruel and unpredictable.

- **In their youth, many were rejected by a group they admired and longed to join—a school or profession, a social class, the military.** Hitler longed to be an artist but failed to get into art school. Saddam Hussein dreamed of being an officer, like his uncle, but was turned down by the military academy. Once in power, Saddam was often seen in military clothing, much like many Nazis who were demoted or rejected soldiers longing to wear a uniform.

- **At the same time, these future tyrants secretly kept a sense of their own special destiny.** Belief in their "mission" fueled a self-centered ambition that pushed other people aside. It both made possible their ruthless climb to the top and helped bring about their downfall.

A question that is frequently asked about the worst tyrants is: were they insane? Their crimes are so horrible that it is tempting to say that no sane person could do such things. But the explanation may not be that simple.

While it is true that many tyrants displayed the same unhealthy personality traits, they are not often the kind that keep a person from operating in daily life. Otherwise, how could these rulers have become so successful? Psychologists and historians who have tried to discover "what was wrong with them" have often pinpointed the same defects. These flaws may warp the way someone thinks and views the world, but they do not keep a person from knowing what he is doing.

Some have argued that tyrants such as Hitler and Stalin were typical narcissists. People with narcissism do not develop a normal relationship to the rest of the world; they stay as self-centered as babies. Only their own pain, their own happiness is real to them; nobody else's feelings matter. Narcissists also have an exaggerated idea of their own importance. They use other people only to prop up the inflated image they have of themselves.

Others have diagnosed tyrants as paranoid: they might have false beliefs about their own greatness or wrongly suspect that others are plotting against them. Such people react violently to any threat to their self-image. Criticism, opposition, even bad news can trigger a rage. It is certainly a description that fits every tyrant: the self-proclaimed great man facing a world filled with enemies who are waiting to betray him if he does not strike first. To make the situation more dangerous, tyrants don't seem to see any difference between politics and personal life: political opponents *are* personal enemies.

Yet despite abnormal traits—and sometimes because of them—these people skillfully manipulate others and accomplish goals many would have thought impossible. It is not perhaps until the end of their lives that they are undone by their flaws. By then, many have lost all touch with reality. Once they stop practicing the cunning self-preservation they used to grab and keep power, their downfall is certain.

The rise and fall of the tyrant is a cycle that has been repeated over and over, in many different parts of the world. Why do people keep allowing tyrants to succeed? Why doesn't anyone stop them? And what do so many people see in the tyrant that makes them think he will act in their interest?

Desperate people often grasp at a "savior," however unrealistic. To the German people after World War I, it seemed one disaster followed another—defeat, soaring prices, unemployment. Many longed for a strong leader to save the day, and for a time it appeared Adolf Hitler was that man. But as they learned to their enormous cost, hero-worship is dangerous when it causes you to stop thinking for yourself.

Sometimes the fear of a greater evil can convince people to put up with a tyrant. But they pay for it in the long run. Nothing frightened the Romans more than the threat of civil war. To avoid it, they tolerated the emperor Nero's wildness and cruelty. The same reasoning has led countries to put up with another nation's tyrant. For years the fear of another world war kept the European powers from standing up to Hitler. Later, British prime minister Winston Churchill was willing to make his "deal with the devil"—the dictator Joseph Stalin—to destroy Hitler at last.

So it is said, a people who feel secure may be led into righteous ways, but a people who feel threatened easily turn to evil.
—Jia Yi, Chinese scholar, on the empire of Qin

In some ways the tyrant behaves like a schoolyard bully. He singles out someone weaker, then pressures others to pick on the unlucky person too. Many of us know better but don't interfere. No one wants to be the next victim.

These stories offer a chilling reminder: tyrants don't operate alone. They are helped into power and encouraged along the path of tyranny by those who hope to gain something. Besides the voters and allies who support him, the tyrant relies on henchmen willing to do his dirty work for reasons of their own— often power or wealth for themselves. But not everyone is willing to back a tyrant, and no amount of force can completely stamp out opposition. The regimes of tyrants have inspired heroic acts of resistance.

The stories that follow take a closer look at some of history's worst tyrants. While there have been many others, these provide some of the starkest portraits of absolute power in evil hands. Some, like Ivan the Terrible, ruled for a lifetime, while a tyrant such as Robespierre held the reins of power for barely a year. Some seized power through deceit or force, some were elected, and some were born to inherit a throne. They justified their crimes in different ways: they ruled by divine right, they fought for the people's liberty, they were saving the country by making it strong. But whatever their route to power or motive for wielding it, they all overstepped the line that separates the responsible use of power from tyranny.

QIN SHI HUANGDI
THE FIRST EMPEROR OF CHINA

An end to the wars was in sight. The 38-year-old king of Qin (*Chin*) was on the verge of bringing all of China's warring states under his control. For centuries, seven kingdoms—Qin, Yan, Zhao, Han, Wei, Qi, and Chu, each with its own ruler and army— had endlessly battled one another. A united China did not yet exist. But that was about to change.

> *A thief steals a purse and is hanged, while another man steals a state and becomes a prince.*
> —Zhuang Zhou, Chinese philosopher

The well-populated state of Qin was known for its harsh laws, its immense army, and its much-feared ruler. King Zhao Zheng (*jhow jhung*) followed in the footsteps of Qin's previous rulers, who had pursued two goals: building a mighty army and farming as much land as possible. With all the surplus grain reserved to feed its soldiers, Qin was transformed into a disciplined and well-fed fighting machine.

King Zheng was ambitious to set Qin above the other kingdoms. At the age of 27 he had started increasing the size of his army, which already numbered at least a million men. Once he was sure it had no equal, he unleashed his chariots, cavalry, and infantry on a brutal conquest of the six neighboring kingdoms. Zheng also put his spies to work, using threats and bribery to break any alliances the other kings might make against him. Agents were sent out to rival states with instructions to "buy those who love gold"—and kill those who could not be bought. Zheng's forces overran one state after another—"as a silkworm devours a mulberry leaf," in the words of one ancient writer.

After 11 years, Qi, the last holdout among the Chinese states, fell to Qin. The cost in human lives had been extraordinary, but a century and a half of war finally had been brought to a halt. Zheng was now the undisputed ruler of all of China. And so, he decided, he needed a new name. Zhao Zheng called his chief minister, his grand councilor, and his chief justice before him at the royal palace.

"I have raised troops to punish violence and chaos," he declared. "With the support of the sacred power of the ancestral temples, the six kings have all admitted their crimes, and order is magnificently restored in all under heaven. Now, if my title is not changed, how will these achievements be praised and remembered by later generations?"

The ministers debated the matter, then turned back to Zheng. "In the past, emperors ruled over a thousand square *li* of territory, beyond which there were lords and barbarians. The emperor had no control over them. Now Your Majesty has raised forces to bring all the lands within the seas under one rule. This is something that has never been done before."

What was needed, Zheng and his ministers agreed, was a title grand enough to match the achievement. Zhao Zheng listened to their suggestions, discarding some and accepting others. At last he settled upon "Sovereign Emperor."

"We are the First Emperor," he announced, "and our successors shall be known as the Second Emperor, Third Emperor, and so on to the ten thousandth generation, and this tradition will continue without end."

With that, Zhao Zheng was transformed into Qin Shi Huangdi—First Sovereign Emperor of Qin.

It was the *di* in *Huangdi* that caught his subjects' attention. The word suggested divine origins. It belonged to legendary wise kings of the past and could only be considered by the most supreme ruler. For the First Emperor, the choice was deliberate: his was to be no ordinary reign.

The First Emperor's enemies would later spread their own story about his origins, which were far from divine. They claimed his father was not the previous king of Qin at all, but a wealthy merchant named Lü Buwei. That story is unlikely, but Lü Buwei had in fact secured the throne for Zheng's father. The emperor's father had been an unfavored prince, largely ignored among his many brothers, when Lü Buwei used his money to finance his advancement to the position of heir.

Zhao Zheng's father ruled only three years before he died. When Zheng inherited the throne of Qin at 13, he was too young to rule a state surrounded by enemy kingdoms. So Lü Buwei, now promoted to royal adviser, made decisions in his name.

Several years into his reign, the young king received a harsh lesson. A plot to topple him from power was exposed, and, worse, his own mother was involved. At 21, Zheng adopted the sword and cap of adulthood and decided it was time to wield power in his own right. He placed the queen mother under house arrest. In a society where loyalty to parents was so important, he could do no more without destroying his own reputation. Zheng then exiled Lü Buwei, who had been suspiciously close to his mother.

The seeds of deep mistrust—and a terrible fear of dying—had been planted in Zheng. They would continue to grow throughout his life, guiding his actions and his reign.

One man surely benefited from Lü Buwei's disgrace—the king's new royal adviser, Li Si. When he saw that Zheng was headed for victory in his war against the six kingdoms, Li Si had rushed to the state of Qin. "Now the king of Qin desires to swallow the world," Li Si told his teacher before saying goodbye. "It is the golden opportunity for traveling politicians. I shall go westward and give counsel to the king of Qin."

Li Si found that the young king listened eagerly to his advice: never share power, and make yourself

LI SI: THE TYRANT'S FRIEND

In Li Si, the scheming grand councilor of Qin, we can see the portrait of an opportunist who helps a tyrant gain power. Li Si nudged the already distrustful Qin towards ruthlessness, hoping to become more powerful himself. His message was always the same: a ruler must be harsh and control people with punishments. Li Si knew that being the right-hand helper of such a ruler would open up almost unlimited power and riches for himself.

The ordinary person misses his chances. The completion of great enterprises consists of taking advantage of weaknesses and ruthlessly exploiting them.
—Li Si

As a young man, Li Si once noticed rats in an outhouse, feeding on filth, running scared whenever the shadow of a human passed over them. He then observed how the rats infesting a granary were fat and confident, unafraid of anyone. "A person's status is just the same as with rats," the cynical Li Si mused. "It simply depends on where you locate yourself."

feared. He showed Zheng the writings of Han Feizi. It was impossible, this philosopher declared, for a ruler "to reward those who cut off the heads of the enemy, and yet admire acts of mercy and compassion." A king should keep his subjects in line with harsh laws and concentrate on two things: increasing his own power and building a strong army.

Zheng, suspicious of others and ambitious for himself, was impressed. "If I could once meet this author and talk to him, I should die without regret!" he exclaimed.

The ruler alone should possess the power, wielding it like lightning or like thunder.
—Han Feizi

He soon got his chance. Zheng's army had been preparing to attack the province of Han. Hoping to avoid war, Han's king sent Han Feizi to Qin as an ambassador. But Li Si was once again whispering in Zheng's ear. "Han Feizi cannot be trusted," he said. "Arrest him."

Zheng did, then changed his mind and ordered that the philosopher be released. But it was too late: Li Si had already fatally poisoned his potential rival.

By now, the kingdoms of Han and Zhao had each fallen to the Qin advance. Three years into King Zheng's campaign to dominate the other states, the crown prince of Yan could see that his small kingdom would be swallowed up next. There was no way his little army could defend Yan's borders against Qin's horde of soldiers, known for their ruthlessness. In desperation, he sent assassins to kill King Zheng.

Two swordsmen arrived at Zheng's court, each holding a box. One contained the head of a Qin general who had run away; this was to demonstrate the prince of

Yan's friendly intentions. The other held the map of a territory in Yan offered as a gift to King Zheng. Hidden inside the rolled-up map, though, was a dagger.

King Zheng was delighted by the news that Yan was giving in without a fight. He dressed in his ceremonial court clothes and ordered a grand assembly of officials in his palace at Xianyang to receive the ambassadors.

Holding their boxes, the two men approached the steps of the king's raised platform. The officials on either side expressed surprise at the pale face and trembling hand of one of the visitors, but the other ambassador assured the king that his companion was just nervous in the presence of royalty. "He is a rustic type from the barbarians of the northern frontier," he apologized. "He has never seen the Son of Heaven."

"Bring me the map," Zheng ordered.

The bolder assassin handed the map to the king, who began to unroll it. As Zheng's eyes scanned down the unraveling scroll, his glance fell on the dagger, exposed for an instant at the bottom. In a flash the assassin grabbed the king's sleeve with his left hand, the dagger with his right, and lunged at Zheng with the weapon.

Zheng jumped backwards, ripping his sleeve off. He tried to draw his sword, but the weapon was long and he fumbled trying to get it out of its sheath. The assassin

The king of Qin, with his arched nose and long eyes, puffed-out chest like a hawk and voice of a jackal, is a man of little mercy who has the heart of a tiger or a wolf. When he is in difficulty, he readily humbles himself before others, but when he has got his way, then he thinks nothing of eating others alive … If the king of Qin should ever get his way with the world, then the whole world will end up his prisoner.
—Wei Liao, a visitor to the court of Qin

chased the helpless king around a bronze pillar while the startled courtiers stared open-mouthed. They were not allowed to wear weapons in the king's presence, and the armed guards at the bottom of the hall could not approach unless Zheng summoned them. Zheng was too terrified to remember to do so.

Zheng's doctor swung at the assassin with his medicine bag. Finally someone shouted, "Put your scabbard behind you, King!" Zheng managed at last to free his sword and defend himself.

The assassins were killed by Zheng's guards, and in a rage the king sent a huge army to crush Yan. But the conquest did not ease his mind. While the royal doctor was rewarded with gold, the memory of the courtiers who had stood silently by never left Zheng.

A transformation was underway in Qin's capital city, Xianyang. With the last of the rival states conquered in 221 BCE, the city had become the capital of an empire. And Zheng—now renamed Shi Huangdi—wanted it to be without equal. Palaces, gardens, and ancestral temples were rebuilt on a grander scale than before. Craftsmen and artisans had been summoned from across the new empire and were busy melting down the thousands of weapons seized from the former states. The metal would make bells and statues for the emperor's royal courts and palaces. On the hills north of the city, overlooking the river Wei, stood newly built replicas of the palaces of the kings Shi Huangdi had defeated.

Xianyang's grandeur would show everyone his power, the emperor reasoned, and its militarily sound location would protect him and his court from enemies. On three sides the city was bordered by mountains or

THE QIN EMPIRE AND THE MAJOR WARRING STATES

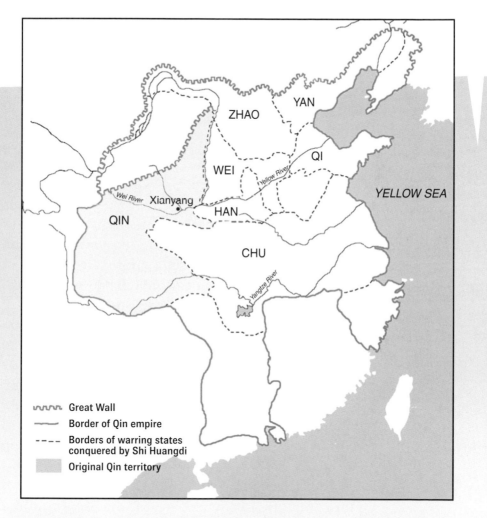

Safe inside the natural stronghold created by mountains and the Yellow River, the state of Qin had plenty of time to build up its military and then begin attacks on its neighbors, without facing the danger of invasion. Qin also had lots of military experience fighting off nomads to the north. In fact, the rest of the Chinese states thought the people of Qin an uneducated group who had more in common with these warlike "barbarians" than with them.

wasteland. The fourth side led down to a valley. There the emperor ordered the building of wide roads that fanned out so imperial troops could sweep outward in any direction across the empire. They wouldn't have to worry about any subjects resisting their arrival, since the emperor had ordered all city walls except those of his capital destroyed.

By royal decree the entire population of the empire had been disarmed—but that did not satisfy Shi Huangdi. People still clung to old loyalties and ties that could interfere with total obedience to the emperor, and these had to go. The First Emperor would no longer tolerate the bonds that had long organized Chinese society, among family members and between feudal lords and the farmers on their land. From now on, one power would control people's lives: the emperor. Loyalty would flow in a single direction, from each subject to Shi Huangdi. Over 120,000 rich families were forced away from their homes and brought to live in the capital. Here, far away from their friends and subjects, the old feudal lords would live under the watchful eye of the emperor.

Even the members of the emperor's own family were kept from getting too powerful. At Li Si's suggestion, Shi Huangdi decided against giving his sons fiefdoms of their own to govern. Li Si advised the emperor to keep the power in his own hands: "Strengthen the trunk and weaken the branches." So the new empire was carved up into 36 districts instead, each of which was run by a governor, a military commander, and an inspector from the royal court who watched over them. Every governor and court official reported to the grand councilor Li Si, who answered only to the emperor.

The new lord of "all under heaven" insisted on unity in all things. For one, Qin's harsh laws were now imposed on all the conquered states. Cruel physical punishments were carried out to deter crime. They also kept anyone from stepping outside his role in Qin's strict hierarchy, which extended from slave to commoner, through some 20 ranks, up to the emperor. And since family members were held responsible for one another, the relatives of a law-breaker were expected to denounce him or her to authorities. If they did not, they were executed along with the condemned criminal "to the third degree"—meaning parents, brothers and sisters, spouses and children.

THE OFFICIAL VERSION

On his tours through the empire, the First Emperor had stone markers set up announcing his virtues and declaring how happy everyone was under his rule. People were reminded to be grateful and obedient by pronouncements such as these:

The August Emperor, sage that he is, has brought peace to the world, never neglectful of his rule.

All under heaven are of one mind, single in will.

He erases doubt and establishes laws, so all will know what to shun.

Evil and wrongdoing are not permitted; all practice goodness and integrity.

The black-headed people are at peace, never needing to take up arms.

In the past, each state had had its own way of measuring, weighing, and writing. That would change too. From now on, "the black-headed people," as Shi Huangdi named his subjects, would use the same weights and measures, pay for goods with the same copper coins, and write in the same language using one script. Travel and trade across the empire were now possible, and—most important to Shi Huangdi—so were taxes. Peasant farmers, no longer dominated by local feudal lords, found themselves under the direct control of the state. They would feel the growing burden of taxes, paid in grain and money. In ever-increasing numbers they would also be drafted into forced labor and military service—all to fund and carry out the emperor's ambitious and endless schemes.

Shi Huangdi may have brought all of China under his power, but another threat lurked on the borders of his new empire. He could not control the Mongol nomads roaming the untamed steppes to the north. To these tribes, China's plentiful farms were easy targets for horseback raids. The nomads carried off whatever their arid homeland could not provide—grain, cloth, ceramics, metal tools. Rather than engage his troops in endless skirmishes with the horsemen, Shi Huangdi devised a solution. His plan was as simple as it was monstrous to carry out: he would wall the intruders off.

So began work on the Great Wall. In the past, China's warring kingdoms had erected their own stretches of wall here and there along the vast northern border, to fend off the nomads and each other. Now, Shi Huangdi sent his trusted general Meng Tian to oversee the connection of them all. Huge fortified towers would be added, linked by walled ramparts. Messengers and soldiers would then be able to move swiftly from tower to tower along the northern border. Safe in the towers, archers could shower arrows onto enemies attacking from below.

For the next 10 years, Meng Tian and the 300,000 forced laborers under his direction would toil on the Great Wall. In the end it would stretch over 3,000 kilometers (2,000 miles), winding over mountains, along steep ridges, and across deserts. Laborers hauled local stone and earth up mountainsides and through wastelands. Some were prisoners of war, disbanded soldiers, or peasants; others were disgraced officials or scholars. Far from home, in the harsh climate of northern China, they built the wall and fought off the nomads at the same time.

No one bothered to count how many people died building the Great Wall, but such a colossal task could only have been completed so quickly at the cost of thousands of lives. Laborers died from the extreme cold, from exhaustion, or from hunger. Often they were buried within the wall itself, which people came to call "the longest graveyard in the world."

Despite the construction of his massive wall, Shi Huangdi remained restless and anxious. After all, there was another, greater enemy he had not mastered: death. Another army of forced labor—700,000 strong—was recruited from across his empire and put to work building a magnificent tomb for Shi Huangdi on Mount Li. His afterlife must be just as splendid as his lifetime, the emperor ordered.

Under the earth, a replica of the world he ruled would be created, a burial chamber holding models of palaces and towers, filled with precious treasures.

THE GREAT WALL:

THE FIRST EMPEROR'S MOST FAMOUS LEGACY

Beginning near China's east coast and stretching westward deep into central Asia, the Great Wall of China covers, with all its branches, 6,400 km (4,000 miles). It is the only human-made object that can be seen from the moon.

The wall we see now is mostly a reconstruction built during the Ming dynasty (1368–1644), but wall-building began during the Warring States period, over 2,500 years ago. The First Emperor of Qin linked the old sections and expanded them. Remnants of the wall built by Qin, mostly stone, can still be seen.

For Shi Huangdi, the wall did more than protect his newly united empire against attack; it also symbolized the order of civilized China. To the First Emperor, China *was* the civilized world; outside was wilderness and chaos. The wall was built well past the populated areas of his kingdom in the hope that the empire would expand to fill the space.

Meng Tian, the Qin general who directed the building of the Great Wall, came to regret the assault his massive construction had made on the natural world. "For what am I being blamed?" he asked when he received the royal order to commit suicide (see page 37). After thinking a long time, he added solemnly, "There is a crime for which I certainly ought to die. I built a wall stretching more than 10,000 *li* from Lintao as far as Liaodong, and so in the course of this I surely could not avoid cutting through the veins of the earth. This, then, is my crime."

Mercury would flow along underground streams to mimic the Yellow and Yangtze rivers. Constellations of jeweled stars would arc overhead. In case thieves were tempted by the riches, deadly crossbows would be rigged to shoot anyone who tried to break in. And over it all, an immense, life-size terracotta army would keep watch to protect the emperor in the next world.

One evening, as guests enjoyed wine at a banquet in the Xianyang palace, an archery captain stepped forward to wish the First Emperor a long life. He praised Shi Huangdi, now emperor for eight years, for bringing peace to the world, and for turning the states of the feudal lords into provinces.

If you preside over them with dignity, [the people] will be reverent; if you are dutiful and loving, they will be loyal; if you promote the good and teach the incapable, they will be mutually encouraging.
—Confucius, giving advice on leadership

The emperor was clearly pleased. But at these words a scholar spoke up. In the past, he argued, dynasties lasted because the ruler assigned territories to his sons and brothers to govern for him. Shi Huangdi, on the other hand, ruled everything himself. "I have never heard of any system not modeled on ancient custom that lasted very long," the man concluded.

When the emperor repeated these words later to Li Si, the grand councilor was quick to pounce. "These scholars study the past in order to criticize the present," he complained bitterly to the emperor. "They confuse and excite the ordinary people."

The time was past when people should be allowed to have their own ideas and criticize their superiors, Li Si advised. Knowledge in the wrong hands was dangerous. Histories written by another state might contradict

LEGALISM VS. CONFUCIANISM

In the Qin era, philosophers and teachers often strove to advise and influence rulers. And two very different philosophies about good government were at odds with each other.

The more traditional Confucianism taught that people have an instinct to be good. This approach grew from the teachings of Confucius, a philosopher from the state of Lu who had lived 300 years before Shi Huangdi. Confucius and his many disciples taught that by following traditions and respecting elders, people can increase their own virtue. A ruler's job is to lead by example.

The newer, more cynical view was called Legalism. It insisted that people are basically bad, and need harsh laws and a strong ruler to keep them out of trouble. The main champion of this way of thinking was Han Feizi, a philosopher from the state of Han, whose ideas spread outside his own kingdom. He advised that too much knowledge in people's hands was dangerous: "In the state of an enlightened ruler, there are no books; law supplies the only instruction."

In the battle to influence the First Emperor's mind, Legalism was the clear winner.

Qin's version of events. The ideas of philosophers often ran counter to Qin's harsh laws. The writings of Confucius were especially threatening. Confucius believed in tradition and duty, especially the duty owed to family. He praised the wise rulers of the past who by their good actions had set an example for the people to follow. His whole outlook belonged to the feudal world Qin had stamped out. Nothing frightened Li Si more than the idea of Confucian scholars plotting rebellion with the former feudal lords.

"Now the emperor has unified all under heaven, marked out black from white, and should be the one and only authority," Li Si argued. His advice was simple and brutal: burn the past.

The First Emperor approved of this view. At his command, countless books of philosophy, poetry, and history—except the official history of Qin—were piled up and set on fire. From now on, only the emperor would have a library, and only a handful of scholars in his pay would ever see it. Anyone who refused to hand over forbidden books within 30 days was sentenced to hard labor. Those caught discussing the banned books were executed. In fact, anyone who "used the past to criticize the present" could be executed, along with his or her family. Subjects were left with only practical books—guides to farming, forestry, and medicine.

The First Emperor did not stop at burning books, however. He continued to send scholars and teachers of all kinds to toil on the Great Wall—the place where countless troublemakers and subjects who failed to please the emperor were put out of the way.

THE TERRACOTTA ARMY

People had always known that the First Emperor was buried somewhere on Mount Li; the story of his colossal tomb was told in Qin's official records. But the location of the tomb was hidden, and grass and trees had covered any trace of its whereabouts.

In 1974, locals digging a well stumbled across an underground pit. The archaeologists who arrived to investigate were amazed as they unearthed first a clay statue

of a soldier, followed by a rust-free bronze sword that still glinted in the sun, then a life-size clay horse! The discoveries continued as news of the find spread.

Just east of the emperor's massive tomb mound, an entire life-size army has now been uncovered, standing guard as real soldiers did outside the capital in the emperor's lifetime. In the largest pit, an infantry regiment stands ready for battle—3,210 foot soldiers, headed by archers. Six chariots, harnessed to terracotta horses, are mounted by charioteers and soldiers. Two of the chariots hold commanders, identified by their headgear, with drums and bells to sound out orders to the troops.

In all, more than 6,000 clay soldiers and horses have been found. The clay army was once equipped with real weapons too, but it is believed these were stolen by the rebels who plundered the tomb when the Qin dynasty fell. To the west of the tomb mound, another bronze chariot and team of terracotta horses stand ready. Their mission was to take the emperor's spirit on its journey in the afterlife. Amazingly, among the thousands of clay soldiers, no two faces are alike; each one is a portrait of a real person.

News of progress on his tomb was often brought to Shi Huangdi, but it did not ease his horrible fear of dying. Two more assassins had tried to kill him. Fearful of his subjects, the emperor no longer let anyone from the conquered states near him. He refused to hear anyone speak of death, and his officials never dared raise the subject. Still, the idea haunted him. Why should he accept the fate of the most common of his subjects? Didn't his name prove that he was above them—divine, in fact? Shi Huangdi and his flattering officials had long proclaimed that the emperor was unique among rulers and mortals. The myth had become so convincing that the emperor seemed persuaded himself: he deserved a special destiny.

A new obsession began to grow in Shi Huangdi's mind—eternal life. He had heard legends of an island in the middle of the sea where people were immortal, and of special herbs that could make a person live forever. Shi Huangdi toured his empire, especially the seacoast, in search of news of these mysteries. He ordered expeditions to sail off the Chinese coast to discover the fabled island of the immortals. Alchemists and magicians were sent on missions to find the herbs of everlasting life. Shi Huangdi began to test one potion after another.

In secret, people whispered about the emperor. Daily he was becoming more arrogant, they said, and no longer consulted his advisers. He had terrified the whole empire with his punishments and executions, and now no one—not even those loyal to him—dared to point out his errors. None of this reached Shi Huangdi's ears, of course. He continued to live surrounded by flatterers who lied to him, telling him what he wanted to hear.

As time passed, those seeking an audience with the emperor began to find it nearly impossible. Almost no one other than his closest attendants saw him any more. The First Emperor had become hidden from his subjects and from most of his courtiers as well.

It was the comments of one of the emperor's alchemists, Master Lu, that had prompted this strange disappearance. The search for immortality had so far failed to yield results, and Shi Huangdi was growing impatient. He was also troubled by bad omens—a fallen meteorite, an anonymous message—that seemed to

THE FIVE POWERS

The First Emperor's belief in magic included an ancient theory that the Five Powers—the elements of water, fire, wood, metal, and earth—follow each other in an eternal cycle. Each ruler finds the source of his power in one of these elements. Since the dynasty before Qin had ruled by the power of fire, Qin reasoned that he must choose the element that overcomes fire—water. Water was linked to the color black, the number six, winter, darkness, death, and ruthlessness.

Since the time of water had come, Qin tried to tap its power. He changed the calendar so that the first month of the year fell in the winter, displayed black everywhere—in clothes and flags—and changed the name of the Yellow River to the Powerful Water. The number six was used as the basis for measurements, and carriages were drawn by six horses. More sinister was Qin's belief that only by being stern and merciless could he fulfill the destiny offered him by the Five Powers.

point to his downfall. The emperor summoned Master Lu before him to report on his progress.

"I and the others have searched for rare herbs and the immortals," Master Lu said, "but we can never seem to find them. Something appears to be blocking us. The magic arts teach that the ruler of men should at times move about in secret so as to avoid evil spirits. When you are in the palace, do not let others know where you are. Once that is done, I believe that the herbs of immortality can be found."

The emperor ordered that his many palaces and towers be connected by raised walkways and walled roads, so he could slip from one to the next unseen. Anyone who revealed where the emperor was at a given moment would be put to death.

Once, from the height of his mountaintop palace, Shi Huangdi noticed Li Si's many carriages and attendants below. He frowned and made a critical comment. One of the royal attendants let Li Si know that the emperor was not pleased, and Li Si scaled back his entourage. When the emperor discovered that someone had repeated his words, however, he was enraged. His attendants were questioned, but no one confessed. Shi Huangdi ordered that everyone who had been within earshot of his remarks was to be executed.

Soon after, Master Lu became afraid that his failure to produce results would cost him his own life. He and another alchemist ran away. News of their escape was the last straw for the emperor. He ordered the imperial secretary to investigate all the scholars in his pay. Terrified, the scholars denounced one another, each hoping to save his own skin. In the end, over 460 were found guilty and executed. Some say they were buried alive.

QIN SHI HUANGDI: FACTS

Born: ca. 259 BCE
Died: ca. 210/209 BCE
Name at birth: Zhao Zheng
Name and titles in power: Qin Shi Huangdi (First Sovereign Emperor of Qin)
Age upon coming to power: 13 (King of Qin); 38 (First Emperor)
Time in power: 36 years
Size of domain: from Qin's 3,000-km (2,000-mile) wall along the Mongolian plateau, south to modern-day Vietnam, and east to the Yellow Sea
Armed forces commanded: over a million troops at the time of the warring states
Number of victims: Unknown. Many thousands died building the Great Wall; thousands of scholars and opponents were also executed.
Defining characteristics: suspicious, terrified of death, convinced of his own divinity
Legacy: Completed the Great Wall. Unified seven kingdoms into what would become China. Established one central government, a single language and script, and one system of measurement. The government structures he put in place would last through all the dynasties that followed.

Only one person was brave enough to speak up and try to save the scholars: Shi Huangdi's oldest son, Fusu. "I fear this will destroy the peace of the empire," Fusu warned his father. "I hope you will think this over."

Little record is left of how Shi Huangdi felt about his sons, but it is clear from this incident that he did not tolerate them contradicting him. For his words Fusu was sent where so many others who had displeased the emperor had gone—to labor on the Great Wall.

Magicians who had been sent to sea to search for the secret to immortality had returned empty-handed. When they learned the First Emperor was touring his kingdom near the coast, they were afraid to approach him with disappointing news. They told him that a giant fish was blocking their way.

Shi Huangdi armed himself with a crossbow and watched for this great fish, which another magician suggested might be an evil water god. As he followed the shore, the emperor suddenly became sick. Just what illness overtook him is unknown, but all the mercury and phosphorous he had consumed while testing his alchemists' potions for eternal life may have poisoned him.

What Shi Huangdi dreaded most was happening: he was dying. The emperor wrote a letter recalling his exiled son from the Great Wall. "When mourning is announced, return to Xianyang with Meng Tian's soldiers and carry out my burial," he instructed the prince. The emperor applied his imperial seal to the letter and handed it to Zhao Gao, the official in charge of messages. Shortly after, still outside the capital, the First Emperor died.

Zhao Gao did not send a messenger to deliver the emperor's last letter. Instead, he took Li Si aside and convinced him they would both be better off if Huhai, one of the emperor's younger sons, succeeded him rather than Fusu. "The eldest son is firm, resolute, warlike, and courageous," Zhao Gao argued. "He is a sincere man and a spirited gentleman, and when he succeeds to the throne, he will make Meng Tian his Grand Councilor."

A chill ran through Li Si. It was true: he would be replaced, and Prince Fusu, as the new emperor, would surely punish his scheming. Together, the two men destroyed Shi Huangdi's letter and plotted to keep his death a secret.

The royal carriage continued its progress through the empire. Food for the emperor was delivered at each stop as usual. But the weather was hot and Li Si knew the smell of the body would soon give the truth away. He ordered the officials accompanying the royal party to load their carriages with dried fish to mask the odor. The emperor had lived hidden from view for so long, and inspired in his followers such fear, that no one dared enter his carriage.

Li Si forged a royal edict announcing that the 21-year-old Huhai was the emperor's heir. He also drafted a new letter for Prince Fusu in the emperor's name, accusing Fusu and Meng Tian of crimes and ordering them both to commit suicide—traditionally a dignified alternative to the execution they would certainly face. By the time the royal caravan reached the capital, Li Si's plot had fallen into place, and the death of the First Emperor was announced.

As Second Emperor, Huhai soon made it clear what kind of reign could be expected from him. An adviser pointed out to him that the artisans who had built his father's tomb knew all about its treasures and its traps for grave robbers. So, as the unlucky workers were setting everything in place for the last time, Huhai ordered that the outer gate be lowered, shutting them in alive. In the tomb with them were all the childless women of Shi Huangdi's harem, whom Huhai had ordered buried with his father.

Li Si and Zhao Gao hoped to manipulate the young

emperor like a puppet, so they flattered his dreams of absolute power. Zhao Gao advised the Second Emperor to begin his reign by arresting governors and commanders across the empire and punishing each for some invented crime. This would strike terror into the empire, he said. After that, Zhao Gao cautioned, it would be best for Huhai to hide his youth and inexperience by keeping himself out of sight, as his father had.

But a weak ruler was no match for the rebellions that were erupting after years of oppression. When news first arrived of garrison troops who had revolted, the Second Emperor had the messenger punished. Messengers who followed learned to keep bad news to themselves. "Just a bunch of bandits," they assured Huhai. "The governors of the provinces are capturing them right now. No need to worry."

In the wave of executions ordered by the Second Emperor, Li Si was killed by the despot he had created. And Shi Huangdi's empire, which he had predicted would last "ten thousand generations," did not survive his death by even four years. In the war that followed, peasant rebels razed his great buildings to the ground. His magnificent capital burned for three months.

Why did the Qin dynasty fall? For one thing, Shi Huangdi's schemes had probably forced as many as 3 million men into his service, leaving few to tend to the agriculture that was the foundation of the empire. The ancient scholar Jia Yi offered a further opinion. The First Emperor used deceit and force to conquer lands and make them his own, but the same tactics could not keep an empire together. Qin was doomed "because it failed to rule with humanity and righteousness, and did not realize that the power to conquer, and the power to hold what has been won, are not the same."

NERO
THE ARTIST-EMPEROR

Rome, 65 CE

A young performer waited anxiously to mount the stage in the Neronian games—contests of skill in music, gymnastics, and riding. He wore the flowing robe of the lyre player, and his sandy hair was arranged in rows of curls, a style more Greek than Roman. He was nervous, but he didn't need to be.

> *Nero ... became emperor ... and through his folly and madness brought the Roman Empire to the verge of destruction.*
> —Plutarch, Greek biographer

Everyone—the judges and the audience—knew who was going to win. This young man would have been sent the victory crown even if he hadn't shown up. For the nervous performer was the emperor Nero, competing in his own games.

Nero had trained hard, and when he took to the stage, he was deadly serious. He followed every rule of the event to the letter, never clearing his throat or wiping the sweat from his brow with a handkerchief. To begin, he recited one of his own poems and was greeted with thunderous cheers.

As usual, the audience was led by Nero's professional applauders; he had more than 5,000 in his pay. They were divided into sections that made different sounds to maximize the effect: the "bees" hummed, the "bricks" and "tiles" clapped. The audience shouted to hear more, so the emperor-actor obliged them. A bodyguard standing by with a lyre handed the instrument to his emperor, and Nero began to play and sing.

The tragic song dragged on, but no one dared to leave. Soldiers often patrolled the audience on the lookout for less than enthusiastic faces—or worse, signs of boredom—and delivered reminders with a sharp whack. The length of Nero's performances was legendary. Stories were told of women who gave birth in the theater, of men who faked their deaths in order to be carried out.

Upper-class Romans were appalled by the sight of their emperor—the commander of the Roman legions, the ruler of the civilized world—living out his dream of acting and singing onstage for all to see. And to make matters worse, the common people cheered him on. Nero knew how to keep the masses happy with lavish shows, which often ended with tokens that could be

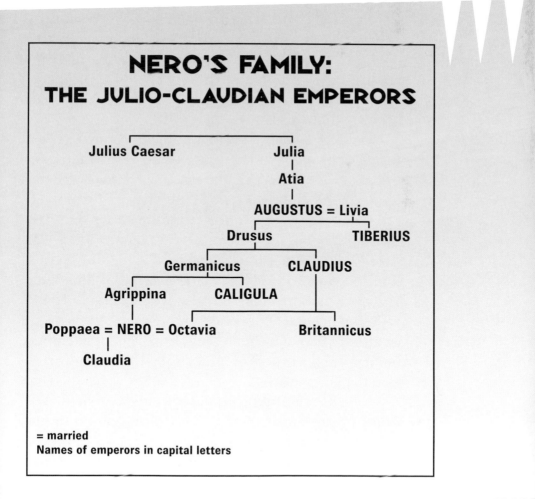

NERO'S FAMILY:
THE JULIO-CLAUDIAN EMPERORS

Julius Caesar   Julia

Atia

AUGUSTUS = Livia

Drusus   TIBERIUS

Germanicus   CLAUDIUS

Agrippina   CALIGULA

Poppaea = NERO = Octavia   Britannicus

Claudia

= married
Names of emperors in capital letters

exchanged for expensive gifts raining down upon the crowds. A lucky spectator might catch a ticket for jewelry, a horse or a slave, even an estate.

For Nero, life was one long stage performance, the Roman Empire his audience. Nothing was sweeter to him than praise and applause. And as long as the show he put on was impressive enough, he knew he could get away with anything—including murder.

The land where Nero was born was the most powerful state in the world. The Roman Empire was vast, its conquered territories a jumble of languages and cultures. Stretching from Great Britain to Egypt, from Spain to the Middle East, it was all held together by legions of soldiers loyal to the line of emperors that had begun with Augustus.

Even for a talented leader, ruling the empire was a tricky balancing act—keeping a lid on revolts and controlling power struggles among the groups that made up Roman society. Each person had a strictly defined place in the social pyramid, from the emperor at the very top down to the lowliest slave. In between were the rich landowners called patricians who dominated Rome's politics and military, the wealthy business class known as equestrians, and the free Roman citizens called plebeians. This last group was the greatest in number, yet held the least power. These farmers, builders, and workers of all sorts paid taxes and struggled to make a living.

Nero's early childhood did not appear to be that of Rome's future ruler. When Nero was three, his father died. His mother, Agrippina, the sister of Emperor Caligula, was banished by Caligula to a small island.

Young Nero's inheritance was confiscated by the emperor and the boy was sent away to live with his aunt, who paid a barber and a dancer to be his tutors.

Then, like a gift from heaven, the family's fortunes changed. Caligula died, and Nero and his mother were recalled to Rome by the new emperor, Claudius. A few years later, Claudius married Agrippina, and she persuaded him to adopt Nero. Eleven-year-old Nero was given the philosopher Seneca as a tutor, and he even became engaged to Claudius's daughter Octavia.

THE BALANCE OF POWER

In imperial Rome, the emperor was the supreme authority, but a wise ruler recognized the delicate balance he must maintain among the other power-holders:

the army: a force absolutely critical to maintaining the emperor's power and Rome's conquered territories. A commander with a legion was a potential threat if he turned on the emperor.

the senate: a wealthy, prestigious group who advised the emperor. The senate's role was reduced under a tyrannical emperor. In theory, the senate approved the choice for a new emperor, but in reality the army and the praetorians had the last word. What many emperors feared most was a plot between the army and a group of senators.

the plebeians: the general population of Roman citizens. The common wisdom was to keep them happy with "bread and circuses"—handouts of food and public entertainment. But commoners also posed the danger of riots. Some cunning emperors knew how to manipulate the crowd by playing upon their emotions; the ruler could then do what he had planned under the guise of "public pressure."

the praetorian guard: the imperial bodyguards. They both protected the emperor and at the same time posed a constant threat: without their loyalty the ruler was exposed and vulnerable.

As a boy, Nero showed promise in public speaking, charming his audiences. Seneca approved and encouraged his young student in this respectable Roman skill. But all the while the palace was a sinister home to grow up in, full of scheming and suspicion. In the thick of the intrigue was Nero's ambitious mother.

Claudius appeared to favor Nero over his own son and heir, Britannicus. But Agrippina, who was determined to see Nero become the next emperor, worried that Claudius might change his mind. Exactly what happened next remains a mystery, but Agrippina was no doubt at the center of events.

Claudius, it is said, arrived very hungry to a meal with Agrippina and was delighted to spy his favorite dish, mushrooms. His taster sampled them, proving them safe to eat. Agrippina then selected one and commented on how delicious it was. Claudius, who had been eyeing the biggest, juiciest mushroom in the center of the platter, now gulped it down, sealing his fate. It was the only one Agrippina had poisoned.

The emperor collapsed and was carried by attendants to his room, where he died shortly afterwards. Agrippina sprang into action. The hours after Claudius's sudden death would be crucial. Nero needed the approval of the senate—and more importantly, the army—to make his power secure. Agrippina knew things could still go wrong.

Nero's mother used all her tricks to keep 12-year-old Britannicus from leaving her side. She clung to him, crying that he was the very image of his poor father. Meanwhile, as Claudius's body was being prepared for burial, Agrippina was sending hopeful words about his recovery to the praetorian guard, the troops responsible for the emperor's safety. She hoped to keep

Nero's proud, cunning mother, Agrippina the Younger. Her great-grandfather, brother, and husband had all been emperors, and she stopped at nothing to put her son in power.

them calm until she was ready, because Agrippina had a winning card up her sleeve: she was the daughter of the much-loved general Germanicus, and she was counting on the loyalty of the army and praetorians now.

Agrippina waited until the astrological signs were favorable before making her move. At noon the next day, she ordered the palace gates to be thrown open and young Nero emerged before the battalion on duty outside. By his side was Burrus, commander of the praetorian guard. A few soldiers glanced around, asking in low mutters where Britannicus was. Burrus spoke briefly to the troops, who cheered. The few who hesitated quickly followed the others' lead as 16-year-old Nero was lifted up and acclaimed the next emperor.

Agrippina, always shrewd about appearances, had the departed Claudius declared a god and made herself his priestess. She had long ago steeled herself to do whatever was needed to place Nero in power. When he was still a child, so the story went, Agrippina had consulted an astrologer about her little boy's future. She was warned that, while her son would become emperor, he would also kill her. "Let him kill me," Agrippina answered, "as long as he rules."

When Emperor Nero stood before the Roman senate and delivered his first speech, everyone was relieved by his sensible and moderate words. He brought no quarrels with him, he said. He would keep personal and state affairs separate. Cases would be judged fairly, there would be no bribing of officials, and the senate's advice would be respected by the emperor. Everyone knew that the reassuring words had been written for Nero by Seneca, who along with Burrus was advising the new emperor. After all, Nero was not yet 17—much too young to govern an empire. It was hoped that the stoic Seneca and a reliable soldier such as Burrus would keep the teenage emperor on a sensible path.

Not long afterwards, the sight of the first coins issued by the new regime gave some Romans a shock. Instead of the traditional image of the emperor's profile, the coins showed Agrippina and Nero face to face, as equals. Was a woman co-ruler of Rome? people asked each other disapprovingly. In fact, the young emperor was dominated by his mother's will on almost every matter. On his first day as emperor Nero had been asked to give a new password to the praetorian guard. "The best of mothers," he had responded.

Whenever her son met with the senate, Agrippina stood unseen behind a curtain, listening to everything. Once, when Nero received delegates from Armenia, she nearly went too far. Entering the room, she was about to join her son on the raised tribunal—unheard of! Luckily, Seneca saved Nero from humiliation. He nudged the emperor to step down and greet his mother before she climbed to the tribunal.

At first Nero seemed to try to keep his promise to be a good ruler. He moved to abolish unfair taxes and showed his distaste for the death penalty. "How I wish I'd never learned to write!" he moaned when signing his first execution order. He even tried to outlaw the killing of gladiators and criminals in public shows, a common practice at the time. But at each step the teenage ruler was frustrated by setbacks. His tax reform was watered down by the senate, then disappeared. Tradition and the public both demanded that gladiators keep fighting to the death. More and more, Nero preferred to dabble in poetry and music rather than undertake the hard job of running an empire.

He was also beginning to bristle under his mother's influence. She scoffed at Nero's poetry writing and disapproved of the dancers and actors who were his friends. In secret, Nero started to show a darker side. He went out at night in disguise with rowdy companions, brawling and robbing people in the streets. One night

Nero led an ambush on a passing senator. Not suspecting who his attacker was, the senator struck back. When he glimpsed Nero's face, he apologized.

It was the worst thing the man could have done. For embarrassing the emperor, the senator was forced to commit suicide—a common death sentence in Roman times. Nero got an early taste of the power he wielded, but he also learned a lesson: from then on he made his nighttime outings surrounded by soldiers and gladiators.

Nero, reclining on a couch at dinner, watched—without appearing to watch—his stepbrother Britannicus, the heir who still haunted him. Agrippina, angry at losing control over Nero, had recently hinted darkly that Britannicus was almost grown up and that he wasn't like certain ungrateful sons who used their power to mistreat their mothers. When Nero had tried to humiliate the shy 13-year-old by ordering him to get up and sing at a banquet, Britannicus had calmly sung about being banished from home and inheritance, and many at the table looked touched. Nero was furious.

Now, from the corner of his eye, Nero observed the boy at the children's table as he was offered a cup. The drink had already been tested by Britannicus's food taster, but as Nero expected, the boy found it too hot. Cold water was quickly brought to cool it down—water that had been poisoned.

Everyone was horrified as Britannicus fell to the floor, convulsing. Some glanced at Agrippina, but the alarm on her face showed that this was not her doing. Nero remarked casually that Britannicus had suffered fits like this since he was a baby; it would pass.

Britannicus's sister Octavia, by now Nero's wife, kept her expression blank. Agrippina too said nothing as Britannicus was carried out. For the first time, Nero had acted on his own, and it could only mean her power was slipping.

NERO: FACTS

Born: December 15, 37 CE
Died: June 9, 68 CE
Name at birth: Lucius Domitius Ahenobarbus
Name and titles in power: Nero Claudius Caesar Augustus Germanicus, Pontifex Maximus (Chief Priest), Tribuniciae Potestatis XIV, Imperator XIII, Consul V, Pater Patriae (Father of the Country)
Age upon coming to power: 16
Time in power: 13.5 years
Size of domain: Roman Empire dominated most of England and Europe, as well as modern-day Turkey, Israel, Egypt, and northern Africa.
Armed forces commanded: at least 300,000 men, including 4,500 praetorian guards and 240,000 in the Roman legions, then the best-trained troops in the world
Number of victims: Total unknown. Besides killing at least nine relatives, Nero executed thousands.
Defining characteristics: artistic, vain, anxious for praise, escapist, fearful, undisciplined
Legacy: Nero brought the Julio-Claudian line of emperors to an end, having executed all possible heirs. His fall turned the Roman armies into a powerful political force. He is remembered as a symbol of extravagance, vanity, and ruthlessness.

The battle of wills between Nero and Agrippina continued to mount. She dismissed his servants; he dismissed her military bodyguard. She complained he was holding back riches that were rightfully hers; he moved her out to a separate mansion, making only brief visits to see her, surrounded by his guards. When Nero wanted to divorce Octavia and marry Poppaea, a beautiful but devious woman, Agrippina refused to hear of it.

Agrippina ... could give her son the empire, but not endure him as emperor.
—Tacitus, Roman historian

Then Nero learned that his mother was spending time talking to various noblemen. Agrippina's enemies encouraged Nero to believe she was casting about for support to overthrow her son. It was easy to spark Nero's fears; hadn't he grown up in the middle of her plots? Without telling Burrus or Seneca, he decided to strike first.

Nero invited his mother to celebrate a festival with him at Baiae, a boat ride from her villa. The two ate and laughed together, and Nero embraced Agrippina before she left. In her honor, he had prepared a sumptuous boat to carry her home—but its canopy was rigged to collapse once she was in the middle of the bay.

At the arranged signal, crew members in on the plot released the weights that brought the canopy crashing down on Agrippina. But she was saved by the high sides of her couch and, wounded, swam ashore. Agrippina pretended to think it was an accident, but Nero was beside himself with terror. His mother would surely retaliate, perhaps even incite the army to mutiny. He sent men to her home to finish the crime.

After the deed was done, Seneca and Burrus set to work controlling the damage. Seneca wrote a letter for Nero to send to the senate, declaring that Agrippina had plotted against the emperor, been discovered, and ended her own life. Burrus directed the captains of the praetorian guard to shake Nero's hand as if he had made a narrow escape. Public celebrations were arranged to thank the gods for Nero's safety.

Still, Nero was afraid to return to Rome. Would the senate and the people play along and welcome him, or would they denounce him as a murderer? When at last he ventured into the capital, he was cheered in the streets. Nero's relief was immense: he was free!

With Agrippina gone, Nero abandoned all self-control. He dressed flamboyantly in the Greek style his mother had always detested, feasted with friends day and night, threw chariot races, and took to the stage himself to perform. Divorcing the respectable Octavia hurt his popularity, but he did not care for long. Reports of rebellions in Britain seemed remote and uninteresting to him, for Nero never bothered to occupy himself with Rome's military conquests. He even avoided addressing the troops for fear that shouting might hurt his singing voice.

Only a handful of incidents hinted that anyone disapproved of the emperor's conduct: graffiti was scrawled at night on public walls, a senator walked out in protest when the senate voted its thanks for Agrippina's death. The rest of the senate turned a blind eye. Putting up with a reckless emperor was better than civil war, they reasoned. Nero was the last of his line, without an heir. If he was removed, they feared, Rome would be plunged into chaos as power-hungry families and commanders fought one another for supremacy.

Nero's recklessness went beyond his involvement in the arts. He had rid himself of his stepbrother, his mother, and his wife, and no harm had come to him.

COMMAND PERFORMANCE

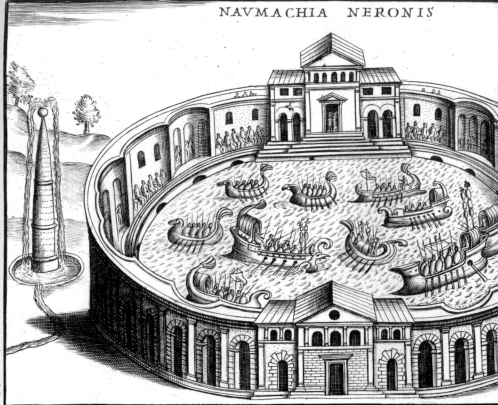

NAVMACHIA NERONIS

Image provided by Fine Rare Prints (www.finerareprints.com)

Nero had one arena flooded with water so the crowds could watch ships in a sea battle. Sea creatures, seals, and bears were released into the water to make the scene more exciting.

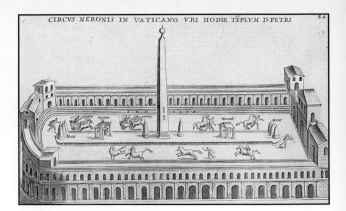

CIRCVS NERONIS IN VATICANO VBI HODIE TEPLVM D·PETRI

Nero built amphitheaters and put on a huge variety of free spectacles for the people of Rome, which made him popular with the crowds. He adored chariot races, gladiator contests, wild animal shows, dramatic plays, and frenzied dances. He also enjoyed making upper-class Romans participate in his shows, pressuring wealthy men and women, young and old, to take part. At Nero's urging, one aristocratic Roman rode an elephant down a sloping tightrope. The emperor also made hundreds of senators and knights fight each other in the arena.

As for plays, the wilder and more sensational, the better. When Nero staged *The Fire*, a house was set alight and the actors were allowed to take home whatever valuable objects they could rescue from the blaze.

At first Nero watched these shows from inside a closed imperial box, peeking through a small window. Later he had the box opened, and finally could not resist taking to the racecourse or the stage himself. Nero shocked Romans by playing parts beneath the dignity of an emperor: slaves, beggars, lunatics, women in childbirth. When playing female roles, he wore a mask with the features of whatever woman fascinated him at the time. Nero's choice of roles sometimes confused onlookers. He once played the Greek hero Hercules gone mad, dressed in rags and tied to the stage with chains. It was said that one of his young praetorian guards rushed onstage to free him.

Nero now became bold about destroying anyone who threatened him—an officer too much admired by the crowd, a nobleman who could trace his ancestry to Augustus as directly as Nero could. To be done with Octavia once and for all, he used his favored method: his former wife was exiled, then killed on the pretext of a false charge.

When Burrus died, Seneca was left alone to restrain the 24-year-old emperor without bringing Nero's anger upon himself. It was a balancing act he found impossible. "If the state is too corrupt to be improved, if it is entirely overwhelmed by evil," he wrote, "the philosopher should not continue to strive in vain." He asked for permission to retire.

Then, while Nero was enjoying a lavish banquet at his seaside villa in Antium, terrible news reached him: Rome was on fire. The blaze had broken out in shops near the Circus. Fanned by winds, it was spreading through the ancient, narrow streets. Nero hesitated at first, but when the size of the disaster became clear, he hurried back. He opened public buildings to shelter the homeless and cut the price of grain to feed those who had lost everything. But once the flames were out, disturbing stories began to spread. Nero had watched the blaze from his palace roof, people said, and found the flames so beautiful that he had called for his lyre and sung one of his own compositions, dressed in his stage costume.

When the last smoldering ruins had been doused, builders and artisans set to work at a furious pace. Construction on a massive scale was underway in Rome's burned-out city center. But the project was not

DID NERO REALLY FIDDLE WHILE ROME BURNED?

So many stories sprang up about Nero that it can be hard to tell which ones are true. And yet the legends show us something important about the real man: how people saw him and what they thought he was capable of.

In the most famous legend, Nero "fiddled while Rome burned" in

Engraved for the Oxford Magazine.

Nero Fiddling, Rome Burning, Pompaja & Agrippina Smiling.

64 CE. The truth is hard to pin down; the Roman historians who recorded the incident all wrote different versions. One said Nero watched the fire from a tower and recited a long poem about the destruction of the ancient city of Troy. Another said he stood on the roof of his palace and sang. A third claimed the emperor performed on his private stage. Only one of the writers admitted that his version was a rumor. But the story endured because—true or not—it painted a perfect picture of Nero's character: unconcerned with the suffering of others and obsessed with his art, which he preferred to real life. As for the fiddle: if he had played anything at all, it would have been his lyre.

new houses for homeless families: it was an immense new palace for Nero. Nero's *Domus Aurea*, or Golden House, was the royal playground of his dreams, never possible until now. Its luxury would consist of something more than gold ornament, of something much harder to come by in crowded Rome: space. The palace would be surrounded by an enormous private park with lawns, forests, an artificial lake, and cascading fountains. The palace entrance would be big enough for a colossal statue of Nero, which would tower 37 meters (121 feet) above his awed visitors. Dining-room ceilings would be equipped to shower flowers and perfumes on the guests of Nero and Poppaea.

Nero was delighted with the plans. "Now at last I can begin to live like a human being!" he commented. But he had not helped his reputation by taking advantage of the fire to build his pleasure palace. Rumors about Nero became more vicious. He not only had watched the giant blaze with glee, people said, but had started it himself! So the emperor quickly found a scapegoat for the fire—a group so unpopular among Romans that he hoped people would be happy to see them punished. He blamed the members of a new religion: the Christians. They were rounded up and cruelly executed, but the rumors about Nero and the fire were not put to rest.

The cost of the Great Fire, the Golden House, and Nero's lavish parties had sent him in constant search of money. His lifestyle was extraordinarily expensive: he never wore a robe more than once; his wife kept a herd of 500 donkeys—all wearing gold shoes—so she could bathe daily in their milk. Heavy taxes and melting down the gold from Roman temples were not enough. So Nero revived a much-hated tradition—treason trials. It was a profitable way to dispose of his enemies, since the emperor could seize the convicted person's property.

Fearful for Rome's future, a group of senators and officers decided drastic action was needed. They plotted to kill Nero at the Circus Games. One conspirator would pretend to approach the emperor with a petition, then pin him down. Another would rush in and stab him. Then Piso, a well-liked aristocrat, would be brought to the praetorian camp to be proclaimed emperor. But the man who was to wield the knife was betrayed by one of his slaves. One by one the conspirators were arrested, tortured, and forced to name names.

At such a court it is a miracle to reach old age, and the feat can only be accomplished by accepting insult and injury with a smiling face.
—**Seneca**, on the state of Nero's court

The terrified Nero turned Rome into a prison: his guard was doubled, troops manned Rome's walls, and access to the city by water was blocked. Soldiers regularly invaded people's homes. The arrests multiplied as Nero lashed out in fear. Lines of chained men were dragged to his gardens to be interrogated, often by the emperor himself. Any link to one of the plotters—a chance conversation, attending the same party—was enough to condemn them. Nero hoped the names of people he hated would come up in these confessions. When they didn't, he often sent his guards to their houses anyway. Both innocent and guilty were exiled, executed, or forced to commit suicide.

Even Seneca, Nero's former adviser, had not found a safe haven. Under torture, someone had named him. An officer of the guard arrived at the philosopher's home as he was dining with his wife and friends to tell him of his death sentence. Seneca faced his suicide with the stoicism he had preached, and chided his companions for crying: "Surely nobody was unaware that Nero was cruel! After murdering his mother and brother, it only remained for him to kill his teacher and tutor."

The Olympic Games had been held in Greece every four years for eight centuries, but that was about to change. Greece was now a Roman province, and Nero ordered that the Games be postponed until his visit. He wanted to compete in them. For his benefit, singing and acting were added to the more traditional athletic contests. "The Greeks alone know how to appreciate me and my art," Nero declared.

Above all [Nero] was carried away by a craze for popularity ... He had a longing for immortality and undying fame.
—Suetonius, Roman historian

Besides the plot on his life, one tragic event after another had plagued Nero. Poppaea had given birth to a baby girl who died within months. A grieving Nero declared the infant a goddess. Then, in a temper tantrum, Nero had struck his wife, who was pregnant again. She died shortly after, and Nero was filled with remorse. Now, sailing to Greece, the emperor left his troubled life and capital behind for escape into a fantasy world.

Nero bribed the best contestants, along with the judges, and had last-minute words with them all to make sure he would win every contest. Still he suffered from stage fright. While acting in a tragedy, he dropped his scepter and was terrified that he would be disqualified. But his co-actor assured him that no one had noticed— they had all been too caught up in his performance. Nero's ambitions overshot his abilities when he insisted on racing a chariot with a team of 10 horses, a dangerous sport. He fell out of his chariot—but still received first prize.

On his return to Rome, Nero paraded through the streets in a chariot, the Olympic wreath on his head. A mantle covered with gold stars was draped over his purple robe. Following his chariot, his professional applauders cheered him: "Hail, Olympian victor! The only victor of the grand tour, the only one from the beginning of time!" It was a ceremony normally reserved for military heroes, but in Nero's mind he *had* just fought for Rome—not on the battlefield, but onstage—and returned triumphant.

Nero was relaxing in Naples when news reached him that Vindex, the governor of a province in Gaul, had rebelled. The emperor appeared unconcerned. When a more serious message arrived later that day, he threatened to punish the rebels but otherwise shrugged it off. In fact, he did nothing for days.

Vindex insulted Nero in public proclamations, but only one remark pierced the bubble of Nero's fantasy world: Vindex called him a bad lyre player. The emperor was roused enough to write to the senate. He asked them to seek revenge on his behalf, as he was unable to do anything because of a sore throat. Urgent messages eventually forced Nero to return to Rome, but he did not address the senate or the people. He did, however, summon some leading advisers to his home—where he broke off their discussions to demonstrate his new water-organ.

Then Nero learned that Galba, the governor of

He who wields power by force does not wield it for long.
—Seneca

THE ROMAN EMPIRE
AT THE TIME OF NERO

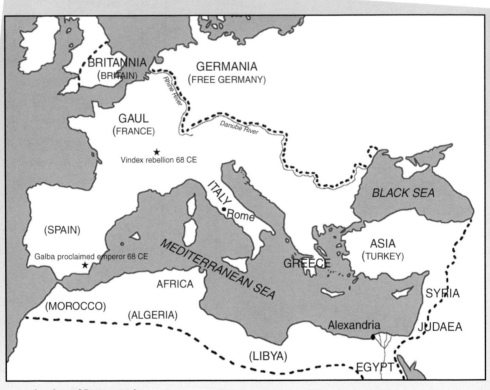

BRITANNIA
(BRITAIN)

GERMANIA
(FREE GERMANY)

Rhine River

GAUL
(FRANCE)

Danube River

★ Vindex rebellion 68 CE

ITALY

•Rome

BLACK SEA

(SPAIN)

★ Galba proclaimed emperor 68 CE

MEDITERRANEAN SEA

ASIA
(TURKEY)

GREECE

AFRICA

SYRIA

(MOROCCO)

(ALGERIA)

Alexandria

JUDAEA

(LIBYA)

EGYPT

– – – borders of Roman territory

Modern names of countries in brackets

The empire Nero inherited was immense, but he took little interest in conquering new territory or even protecting his empire's frontiers.

Spain, had also rebelled. This time Nero fainted. When revived, he cried out that all was over. But still he did nothing, never taking command of the legions that remained loyal to him. The joint commanders of the praetorian guard began to wonder if their emperor was a lost cause. Finally, Nero remarked to friends while leaving a banquet that he had hit upon a plan. He would travel to Gaul and weep before the rebel troops. This would win back their loyalty. He would then sing them songs of victory, which he must leave at once to write.

While Nero refused to take action, rumors spread: The emperor intended to use the rebellions as an excuse to plunder the provinces, then execute all the army commanders and provincial governors as members of a single conspiracy. He was going to poison the entire senate at a banquet—or set fire to Rome again!

When another feast was interrupted with news that more armies had rebelled, Nero tore up the dispatch and overturned the table. In a panic, he invented and discarded plan after plan. He would throw himself on Galba's mercy. He would beg the people's forgiveness; perhaps they would let him govern Egypt? He might persuade the praetorian guard to flee with him by ship. Tomorrow he would decide. He left his Golden House to spend the night at his mansion on the outskirts of Rome.

When Nero awoke at midnight, he was alone. He searched for his bodyguards and friends, but they were gone. At last he found an attendant named Phaon, who offered to hide him at a villa outside the city. Nero pulled a cloak over his head and left immediately with Phaon and three other members of the household. Once at the villa, the four urged the emperor to kill himself. He directed them to begin digging his grave, and as they did so, he wept and repeated, "What an artist dies with me!"

A messenger arrived with a note for Phaon. Nero grasped it and read that the senate had declared him a public enemy and he was to be punished in the ancestral manner. "What does that mean?" he asked, and heard the chilling answer: he was to be led naked through the streets with his neck in a yoke and beaten with rods.

Nero picked up two daggers, then hesitated. Perhaps someone else might set an example by killing himself first? he suggested. No one volunteered. Finally, at the sound of horses' hooves outside, Nero stabbed himself with the help of one of his companions.

The last of the Julio-Claudian Caesars was dead at 30. And with his death Romans were plunged into the civil war they had dreaded above all. Backed by different legions, three new emperors followed each other in quick succession. Each one was toppled within months. Meanwhile, the armies of Rome's provinces had realized how powerful they were, and they would continue to struggle against one another for centuries to come.

IVAN THE TERRIBLE
CZAR OF ALL RUSSIA

Russia, 1570

On a cold January morning the townspeople of Pskov braced themselves for the assault they knew was coming. Thousands of black-robed horsemen were already riding towards this city not far from Russia's northwest border. These were the *oprichniki*, the special guards of Czar Ivan IV.

News had traveled quickly to Pskov of the destruction the czar's forces had brought to nearby Novgorod. The Novgorodians had always shown an independent spirit, but the previous fall stories had reached Ivan's court in Moscow: a plot was brewing among the nobles and officials of Novgorod. Some said they wanted to replace Ivan with another prince. Others claimed the Novgorodians wanted to hand over their city to Russia's enemy, the Polish king. Ivan didn't wait to find out if either story was true. His vengeance on Novgorod was swift and ruthless. The czar assembled thousands of his *oprichniki* and set off for the city, laying waste to town after town along the way.

He who resists power, resists God.
—Ivan the Terrible

Once the czar's forces had reached their destination, Ivan attended Mass in the cathedral. He rejected the archbishop's welcome but accepted an invitation to dinner. During the meal, Ivan suddenly ordered his *oprichniki* to arrest the archbishop and all his servants. Hasty trials of Novgorod's nobles, priests, and officials followed, in Ivan's camp outside the city. While Ivan looked on, the accused were tortured until they confessed to treason. Many of the supposed traitors were set on fire, then taken by sled to the frozen river and plunged through the ice. Others were marched back to Moscow for a public execution.

For six weeks Novgorod was sacked. The *oprichniki* emptied the churches of precious icons and valuables, including the cathedral's handsome doors, which were torn off. Ivan's troops fanned out through the streets, looting shops and homes. Citizens who refused to hand over their money or goods were killed where they stood. Thousands died in the pillaging.

Their work done in Novgorod, at Ivan's order the *oprichniki* mounted their horses and set off for Pskov, where they planned to act out the same grim scenes. Still some distance from the city walls, however, Ivan and his men saw a figure waving its arms. Coming closer, they could see it was a thin man in rags, barefoot in the snow.

The man's name was Nikola. Ivan knew of such *yurodivyi*, or "holy fools." Leaving their homes and families, these people lived apart like beggars, raging against the evils of the times. Some thought the *yurodivyi* were insane, but many Russians believed they were special and could even foresee the future.

Ivan's henchmen were about to brush Nikola aside, but Ivan reined in his horse and ordered the army to halt. Nikola boldly stepped forward. Lifting his bony arm in the air, he issued a stern warning: a terrible fate awaited Ivan if he raised his hand against Pskov. As the hermit spoke, Ivan stared silently, his breath white in the winter air.

In the hush that followed, the *oprichniki* waited for a blow from Ivan's staff to knock the holy fool down. But none came. Then Ivan gave an abrupt order for the army to retreat. Amazed, his henchmen obeyed.

Those who knew Ivan well were not surprised. Any other Russian subject would have been put to death for speaking in such a manner to Ivan *Grozny*—"The

Terrible." But the holy fool struck a chord with the czar, who was a strange mixture of cruelty and religious devotion. Over the next few days a handful of Pskov's nobles and officials would be arrested, but the city itself was spared.

Ivan became Grand Prince of Moscow when he was three years old, and he would later have no memory of becoming a ruler: "I grew up on the throne," he remarked. The child prince also had no idea of how vast a land he had inherited. Russia in 1533 was already an enormous domain—twice as big as England, France, and Spain put together.

This immense territory was dotted with cities whose princes ruled the surrounding countryside. The princes competed with one another, but they were all dominated by the Tatars, invaders from the Asian steppes southeast of Russia. These overlords were descended from the Mongol hordes of the legendary conqueror Genghis Khan. The Tatar ruler, the Khan, chose Russia's princes and demanded they pay tribute to him.

Over time, Moscow had become powerful among the Russian cities, as it took over the weaker settlements nearby. The Moscow prince was served by a household of lesser princes from the lands he now commanded, as well as by the noble families who had advised Moscow's rulers for generations. To these nobles, called boyars, the prince granted estates farmed by peasants. In return, he expected the nobles to be loyal and serve in his army.

But a child on the throne posed a problem. Although Ivan had become Grand Prince when his father, Vasilii, died, it was in name only; someone else

The Russian czar and his noble advisers, the boyars. Ivan took away many of the boyars' traditional powers in his mission to make the czar the one and only authority.

would have to rule for him until he grew up. Ivan's mother Elena, her relatives, and a council of boyars appointed by his late father took charge.

Ivan lived with his mother in a palace inside the Kremlin, the walled citadel that was home to Moscow's princes. He rarely saw the world outside. The priests who were his tutors read the Bible with him, and gave

Ivan books on history and religion. He adored the stories of biblical kings and saints. He was also fascinated by the rituals of Russia's solemn church services, where icons and incense created an aura of mystery. For company, Ivan had his deaf-mute younger brother, Yurii, and the boys' nurse, the sister of his mother's closest adviser.

Then, as Ivan turned eight, his protected world fell apart when his mother died suddenly. Up until then, Ivan had been only dimly aware of the scheming that filled the boyar council, as noble families plotted against one another to increase their own power. Men disposed of their rivals by inventing charges of treason against them; soon after, the tables would be turned and the accuser arrested. Now nothing stood between Ivan and these ambitious boyars, and their treatment of the young prince quickly changed.

Among the boyar clans, the Shuiskii family began to win the fight for control. To secure their position, they needed to keep a tight grip on the orphaned prince. Ivan's nurse was dragged away before his eyes, and her brother, Elena's old friend, was thrown into prison.

The boyars found Ivan useful as a figurehead. When important visitors came, Ivan would be dressed in his royal robes and the boyars would kneel before him. Nervous and wide-eyed, the boy would try to look like a serious prince. But as soon as the guests were gone, he was stripped back down to his usual tattered clothes and ignored. Sometimes he and his brother were left unfed.

As Ivan roamed unnoticed through the halls of the Kremlin, he glimpsed many things he was too young to see: acts of cruelty, even torture, as the clans fought one another. Who would teach him to rule? Surely not these men. But Ivan did learn something: never trust the boyars.

Much about the rest of Ivan's childhood is uncertain, but some say that at age 13, Ivan took a bold step. The more he read about the biblical kings, the more he resented the disrespect the boyars showed him. Wasn't he God's chosen leader, placed on earth to act in His name? Ivan began to rehearse in his mind the action he was about to take.

His chance came shortly after Christmas, while he presided over a banquet. The boyar guests feasted and boasted loudly, ignoring the prince, who sat flanked by guards at the head of the table. Suddenly the young prince stood up from his place of honor. It took a moment for the rowdy dinner guests to notice, then a hush fell over the table as Ivan began to speak. His firm voice surprised them.

Our boyars governed the country as they pleased, for no one opposed their power ... I adopted the devious ways of the people around me, I learned to be crafty like them.
—Ivan the Terrible

The nobles present had taken advantage of his youth, Ivan said gravely. They had abused their power by robbing the country's workers and peasants, and by imprisoning innocent people. Ivan's heart pounded as he spoke, but he forced himself to look each boyar in the eye. They were all guilty, he declared. But he would, as their prince, spare the rest of them if the worst of their lot was executed— Prince Andrei Shuiskii.

In the seconds that followed, Ivan felt more fear than he had in all the uncertain years he'd lived within the Kremlin. Would the guards do as he said? Or would Ivan himself be dragged away at Shuiskii's order? No one at the long table moved or spoke. They eyed one another. Who among their number would raise his hand openly against the prince? Nothing happened. Then the guards stepped forward, grabbed Prince Andrei by the arms, and pulled him out of the room.

Ivan's mother's family, the Glinskiis, were overjoyed by the Shuiskiis' disgrace. It was their turn now to dominate the Moscow court. They treated Ivan better than the Shuiskii family had, although they continued making decisions in the prince's name. That was fine with Ivan. He would not take such a bold action again for years. But he would never forget the time he spent as a powerless child in the boyars' hands, and he would never forgive them.

The coronation of 16-year-old Prince Ivan in the Kremlin's Uspenskii Cathedral was a grand occasion. No such ceremony had taken place in living memory. Ivan was finally ready to take command himself, and he had decided to assume a new title. From now on he would be *czar* —a name that came from the Roman "caesar"—of all Russia. People suspected this meant Ivan had ambitions to expand his domain. They were right. Ivan had begun to look past his father's territories and dream of a grand, unified Russia, with its ruler in Moscow.

In the cathedral a solemn procession of courtiers, all clothed in gold and brocade, made its way to the altar. There the Metropolitan—the head of the Russian Orthodox Church—presented Ivan with a jeweled cross and a golden peaked crown trimmed with fur. A prayer was chanted wishing the czar a long life. The priests had based the ceremony on Byzantine traditions, but the last coronation had taken place so long ago that they misread some of the instructions. Instead of throwing coins to the crowds, Ivan himself was showered with gold coins by his brother Yurii.

Days later, Ivan made a second announcement: he intended to marry. And he wanted a Russian bride rather than a foreign princess; he might not get along with a foreigner. His choice was Anastasiya Romanovna,

IVAN THE TERRIBLE: FACTS

Born: August 25, 1530
Died: March 18, 1584
Name at birth: Ivan Vasilyevich
Name and titles in power: Grand Prince of Moscow; Ivan IV, Czar and Grand Prince of all Russia
Age upon coming to power: 3 (Grand Prince); 16 (Czar)
Time in power: 50 years
Size of domain: Nearly 2.5 million sq km (1 million square miles) when Ivan was crowned. Ivan aggressively expanded his territories eastward throughout his reign.
Armed forces commanded: Special corps, the *oprichniki*, of up to 6,000 men; palace infantry of 3,000 musketeers. Estimates for Ivan's army on his campaigns range from 30,000 to 300,000.
Number of victims: Estimates vary. Ivan admitted to more than 3,000. The sack of Novgorod alone killed up to 15,000.
Defining characteristics: well-read, deeply religious, suspicious, easily excited and angered
Legacy: Expanded Russia's territories and unified the country under one ruler. Laid the groundwork for Russia's future czars to become supreme rulers with unlimited power.

a girl of Ivan's age. The Metropolitan and the boyars were satisfied, since Anastasiya's family had no enemies at court. Ivan was surprised by the deep affection he soon felt for his new wife. He called her his "little heifer."

Despite his lofty title, Ivan was still far from wielding personal control over his country's fate. Tradition held that all his decisions must be approved by the council of boyars, with whom he met almost daily. "The czar has directed and the boyars have agreed" were the words beginning every royal decree. The teenage czar looked for guidance from a man he had grown to trust, a priest named Sil'vestr. The priest reminded the young ruler to use mercy and to fear God's final judgment of his reign in the afterlife. Ivan listened in awe. He had high-minded hopes of bringing order and fairness to the country for which God had made him responsible. Besides Sil'vestr, Ivan turned for help to Andrei Adashev, a young officer and one of the few boyars Ivan trusted.

But Ivan's ambitions were suddenly interrupted. On the heels of the young czar's coronation and marriage came a disaster. That summer, a fire started among the wooden buildings of medieval Moscow, and soon the whole city was ablaze. Many churches and countless icons were destroyed. Even parts of the Kremlin burned. Thousands of people died.

The survivors cast about for an explanation, or at least someone to blame. It was a divine punishment for the wickedness of Moscow's citizens, said a few, including Sil'vestr. But others blamed the boyars, in particular the Glinskii clan. While in charge, the family had earned a bad reputation among the country's workers, merchants, and peasants. Some Glinskiis extorted money from commoners, and they made sure people's pleas for justice did not reach the young czar.

The rumors quickly became vicious. Some were bizarre. Many Russians were superstitious, and now it was said that the hated Glinskii family had used black magic to start the fires. Ivan's grandmother, Princess Anna Glinskii, must be a witch, people whispered. She had flown over the city, setting it alight. Angry crowds swarmed the courtyard outside the Kremlin cathedral, shouting for the suspects. All but one of the Glinskiis had already fled the city. Alone, Ivan's uncle Prince Yurii Glinskii tried to find sanctuary inside the cathedral. The mob dragged him back outside and stoned him to death, then looted his home and attacked his servants.

Ivan now knew the terrible power of a mob. Although he could not prove it, he was sure someone had put them up to it—rival boyars who hated his mother's family. It was a vivid lesson in how the crowd could be swayed against someone powerful—a lesson he would later remember.

Ivan was determined to live up to the name of "czar," and he would do it by making Russia a formidable power. This meant first casting off the Tatars once and for all. Moscow's old masters, now weakened, had withdrawn to their fortresses just outside Russia's borders. It was time, Ivan decided, to take charge of his army.

In 1552, Ivan mustered his troops and rode with them east from Moscow to lay siege to the Tatar stronghold at Kazan, on the Volga River. The czar spent the campaign either praying for victory in a chapel in the army's camp or riding among the troops under his banner in order to inspire them. Once the Russians' cannons had shattered Kazan's outer walls, the Tatars surrendered within hours.

RUSSIA UNDER
IVAN THE TERRIBLE

WHITE
SEA

FINLAND

BALTIC SEA

Novgorod

Pskov

LITHUANIA

Aleksandrova
Sloboda

Moscow

Kazan

POLAND

TERRITORIES
OF THE
TATAR KHANS

Volga River

BLACK SEA

CASPIAN
SEA

– – – borders of Russia in 1533, when Ivan became Grand Prince

areas conquered by Ivan during his reign

Ivan waged war against his Polish and Lithuanian neighbors in an effort to expand his domain, but he had more success conquering territory to the east—at the expense of Russia's former overlords, the Tatar khans.

On his return home, Ivan was met by a breathless messenger from Moscow. Anastasiya had given birth to a boy, Dimitri. Ivan was so overjoyed he gave the messenger his own horse and cloak. The czar was close to his wife, who, like Ivan, was deeply religious. But she was much more patient and gentle than her husband, who had turned into a headstrong and excitable young man.

Ivan sped homeward to find Moscow celebrating both his military victory and the birth of an heir. But the rejoicing was brief. In the spring of 1553, news spread like wildfire through the Kremlin that the 22-year-old czar was seriously ill. Ivan's condition, probably severe pneumonia, grew rapidly worse. Soon he could no longer leave his bed. Death was not far off, he was sure, and he would be leaving behind a five-month-old son. Ivan summoned the boyars to his bedside and demanded they swear an oath of loyalty to Dimitri. Ivan's trusted favorite Adashev and Anastasiya's relatives quickly kissed the cross to seal their oath. But to Ivan's horror, the rest of the boyars hesitated, then left to debate the matter outside his room.

While Ivan lay feverish and helpless, the boyars argued. Some of them would be glad to serve the infant czar but not his mother's family. Others worried that they would be plunged back into the power struggles of Ivan's own childhood. What about crowning Ivan's cousin, Prince Vladimir, instead, they suggested. At least he was a grown man.

In the end the boyars agreed to swear loyalty to Dimitri. And a lucky thing for them, too—Ivan soon got better. But the crisis left a deep impression on his already suspicious mind. Were the boyars all traitors who would turn on him the moment he showed weakness?

As time passed, Ivan's imagination turned the boyars' hesitation into a full-blown plot to murder his son and replace him with another prince. Traditions and laws prevented Ivan from punishing the conspirators as he would have liked. In order to do so, trials would be needed, and they would be conducted by the boyars themselves. The Metropolitan could step in and ask the czar to pardon anyone convicted. Besides, talking about who the next czar might be was not treason, or even a crime—not yet, anyway.

The answer, Ivan decided, must be to increase his own power, to become the one and only ruler. He paid a visit to a monk who had once advised his father. "How is it possible," Ivan asked, "for a czar to rule mercifully and at the same time keep his ungrateful subjects obedient?"

"If you want to be an all-powerful ruler," the monk replied, "do not keep a single adviser who is wiser than yourself, for you as czar are better than all. This way you shall hold all men in your hands."

The words fell like seeds on fertile ground. Ivan was ready to cast off the chains restraining him. No earthly power should hold back a czar. Didn't he have the God-given right to punish the wicked and reward the good? It was not only the Tatars who stood in the way of Ivan's dream of a great Russia under his command—the boyars themselves would have to be swept aside.

Once Ivan had recovered from his illness, he decided to make a difficult pilgrimage to a monastery in the north to give thanks for his life. He insisted on bringing Anastasiya and their baby son with him. No one could talk Ivan out of his plans, and Dimitri did not survive the journey. It may have been another such harsh pilgrimage six years later that fatally weakened Anastasiya. The doctors were baffled by her illness, and Ivan watched helplessly as the gentle wife who had now borne him six children grew sicker.

Anastasiya's death in 1560 left Ivan desperate. With growing alarm, the boyars heard the czar's anguished sobs echoing through the Kremlin corridors. People said Anastasiya had eased Ivan's suspicions and softened his anger. Now the czar was sure she had been poisoned by those who resented the favor he had shown her family. The scheming boyars had bewitched her, had denied her medicine, he cried. Ivan's dreams for the country slipped to the back of his mind. Now he saw plots everywhere, and felt only rage.

It was not long before Ivan turned on his former favorites, Adashev and Sil'vestr. Suddenly he decided it was they who had been the chief conspirators during his illness. They were just as bad as the other "traitor-boyars," he fumed, always working against him. "You and the priest decided that I should be the sovereign only in words, and you in fact," Ivan accused Adashev. He banished them both, along with their families.

Another friend, Prince Andrei Kurbskii, fled into self-imposed exile to escape Ivan's growing suspicions. The "plot" against Ivan's son, Anastasiya's death, the boyars' arrogance—for Ivan they were all blurring together. "Why did you separate me from my wife?" Ivan wailed in a letter to Kurbskii. "If only you had not taken from me my young wife … If only you had not stood up against me … Then none of this would have happened."

Russia was about to enter a reign of terror. But in Ivan's mind, it was the boyars who were responsible, not him.

LETTER TO A TYRANT

None of Ivan's subjects would have dared to tell him what they really thought of him—with one exception, someone who was far enough away to speak his mind freely. In 1564, one of Ivan's favorite generals, Prince Andrei Kurbskii, fled to Russia's enemies in Lithuania. From this safe haven, Kurbskii wrote boldly to Ivan, accusing him of becoming a tyrant and abusing his power. "Why have you conceived against your well-wishers and against those who lay down their lives for you unheard-of torments and persecutions and death ..." Kurbskii wrote in one letter. "What guilt did they commit before you?" And in another he told Ivan, "The czar himself ought to be the head of the body and he ought to love his wise counselors as though they were his own limbs."

Ivan wrote back, quoting the Bible to defend himself. "Did I ascend the throne by robbery or armed force of bloodshed?" Ivan wrote angrily. "I was born to rule by the grace of God." A nation needed a strong ruler with absolute power, he argued. The alternative was "rule by many," and that meant chaos.

As for his cruelty, Ivan told Prince Kurbskii, it was up to the czar to "save with fear." His job was to deliver "mercy and gentleness for the good; for the evil—fierceness and torment." He criticized Kurbskii for not returning to Russia. "And if you are just and pious, why do you not permit yourself to accept suffering from me?" Kurbskii did not take up the invitation.

Ivan surprised many at court when he remarried within a year of Anastasiya's death. But perhaps it was a good thing, some reasoned. His wife might help control Ivan's behavior, which was becoming ever wilder and more unpredictable.

Then, in December 1564, the czar, his children, and his new wife suddenly left the city. This was clearly no pilgrimage; Ivan had taken his entire treasury and a large armed escort. The mood in Moscow was fearful and tense through the winter as citizens waited nervously for an explanation.

In January, two letters arrived. One was addressed to the boyars, the other to the people of Moscow. To everyone's shock, Ivan announced that he was abdicating the throne. His letter to the boyars accused them of treason and of exploiting the people during his childhood. But he assured the common people that "he had no anger against them."

The boyars quickly grasped that this was an appeal over their heads to the crowd. Common Russians had good reason to fear the anarchy of a state without a leader. The country had been at war with Lithuania ever since Ivan had launched another campaign to expand Russia's borders. A tug-of-war for power among the boyars now would mean chaos. Russia might even be invaded by its enemies.

When the letter to the people was read out in public, merchants and workers begged for Ivan's return and swore that they would help punish any traitors. "Do not abandon us to be devoured by the wolves!" they pleaded.

A group of boyars and priests set out for Ivan's new residence in Aleksandrova Sloboda, 100 kilometers (62 miles) northeast of Moscow. They were disturbed to find that it looked a lot like an army camp. Surrounded by log-and-earth walls, it was heavily defended by troops. The anxious visitors were brought by armed escort before the czar.

Ivan accepted their petition for his return on two conditions. First, he demanded the right to punish traitors as he saw fit, without interference, and to take their property. The delegation had dreaded and expected this, but the second condition surprised them. Ivan would divide Russia in two. One half would become the *oprichnina*, a domain under his complete control. It would include Russia's most abundant lands and wealthiest towns. The rest of the country would be governed in the traditional manner. The name "oprichnina" puzzled some; in the past it had been used to describe the land given to a widowed princess. But to Ivan it was fitting. Even though he had remarried, he often grieved that he was an orphan and a widower, alone in the world.

The boyars could see no choice but to agree. Ivan returned to Moscow, where he declared a state of emergency. He recruited men for the *oprichniki*, a special force of bodyguards loyal only to him. Each candidate's family background was carefully checked, and no relative of any hated boyar was accepted. Ivan moved out of the Kremlin into a Moscow stronghold safe inside the *oprichnina* boundaries. Behind its stone walls, the new troops lived around Ivan like monks, and Ivan ruled them like their abbot, ringing the bells that called them all to church at 4 a.m.

Everywhere in his new domain, Ivan took lands away from princes and boyars and gave them to his *oprichniki* henchmen. Those whose lands were seized were sent to monasteries or to distant parts of the kingdom, far from their friends and supporters.

The division of the country made life confusing. For instance, some Moscow streets were within the *oprichnina*, others not. If their parents lived outside the *oprichnina*, Ivan's *oprichniki* had to stop visiting them. Furthermore, they had to swear an oath not to eat, drink, or speak with any of the old nobles. The penalty for oath-breaking was death. The *oprichniki* understood that their power depended upon complete loyalty to Ivan; it could be snatched away again in a flash.

THE TERRIBLE IVAN

From the 1560s on, Ivan became known as Ivan Grozny, a name usually translated into English as "Ivan the Terrible." But *Grozny* actually means something closer to "awe-inspiring." The name was used even more frequently after his death.

One legend about Ivan told of the wife of one of the Tatar khans (Russia's old enemies) who heard that the baby Ivan had been born with two teeth. "With one he will devour us," she told a Russian envoy, "and with the other he will devour you."

Ivan did not mind this reputation. His subjects should fear him, he believed; that would make them obedient. Yet at the same time, Ivan longed to be loved by the common people. After the sack of Novgorod, for instance, the *oprichniki* began to set up scaffolds and instruments of torture in Moscow's marketplace, and 300 nobles were brought out. Terrified, the people of Moscow hid, but Ivan, dressed in black, rode out on his black horse and called the crowds back to watch. He was not angry at them, he assured them, only at the traitors. But Ivan's victims were often scapegoats for his own crimes. With these public displays, he could show the crowd their czar stamping out corruption in government.

The *oprichniki* were easily recognized by their black robes and black horses. They hung a dog's head from their saddles and carried a broom in their quivers, to show that they bit fiercely then swept traitors away. Underneath their somber costumes were the expensive clothes their new riches had bought them—and their swords.

His corps of loyal troops in place, Ivan attacked the boyars with a vengeance. Trials for treason were held, with Ivan deciding both the verdict and the sentence. Convicted boyars were executed along with their sons, so that the clan would die out, and entire families were condemned. No one must be left to avenge the victims, Ivan reasoned, or even to pray for them. This brutal treatment also served as a warning to everyone else.

A year after Ivan's triumphant return to Moscow, the nobles who remained sent a petition to their czar, begging him to stop the trials and executions: "Most radiant czar, our sovereign! Why do you order our innocent brothers to be killed? We all serve you faithfully … [yet] you have set your bodyguards on our necks, and they tear our brothers and kinsmen from us." Ivan was surprised by the protest, then angry. Everyone who had signed the petition was imprisoned. Some were flogged, others had their tongues cut out, and the ringleaders were executed.

Ivan's drastic measures failed to make him feel safe. Worse, they bred rebellious ideas among his subjects. Whispers about replacing the czar with his cousin Prince Vladimir reached Ivan's ears. But was there in fact a conspiracy, or had Ivan become so paranoid that loose talk was enough to make him lash out? Historians are not sure. In any case, Ivan's *oprichniki* were once again set in motion. Federov, a wealthy boyar and the most powerful of the suspects, was exiled. The *oprichniki* raided his lands, destroying everyone who lived there by sword or by burning them in their cottages.

Ivan interrogated the other conspiracy suspects himself. "Which one of the boyars is a traitor?" he would bark at a man being tortured, then supply a list of names for him to choose from. Confessions in hand, Ivan ordered immediate executions. No time was allowed for victims to pray for their souls. Death by burning or freezing were among his favorite sentences, as Ivan tried to imitate the punishments of hell. Victims were not buried, either, so that they would be shut out of heaven. The czar's revenge was meant to follow people into the afterlife.

Ivan next accused Federov of wanting to seize the throne. The anxious boyar was summoned back to Moscow and brought before Ivan. To Federov's surprise, the czar ordered that the boyar be dressed in royal robes of gold and brocade. Then, standing up from his throne, Ivan invited Federov to take the seat himself. Federov stiffly obeyed. Ivan next handed him the royal staff, set with enormous gems, which the czar always carried. *Oprichniki* and courtiers watched in silent expectation. They knew Ivan loved dramatics— and symbolic punishments.

Ivan bowed low before Federov. "Now you have what you sought and aspired to," he said. Then, rising quickly, he added, "Just as it is in my power to place you on this throne, so it is also in my power to remove you."

This cruelty bred such a general hatred, distress, fear, and discontentment through his kingdom that there were many practices and devices how to destroy this tyrant, but he still did discover their plots and treasons by [promoting] all the rascaliest and desperate soldiers he could pick out.
—Jerome Horsey, English envoy to Ivan's court

As Ivan spoke, he drew a knife out from under the folds of his clothes and stabbed Federov. One by one, the *oprichniki* circling the throne did the same. The "false czar" of Ivan's nightmares was destroyed—but his fears would not be eased for long.

THE MAN AND THE LEGEND

It can be hard to separate fact from fiction in the story of Ivan—so many bizarre tales were told about him both during his lifetime and after. Whether or not they are true, the stories do show how Ivan was both feared and strangely admired, inspiring horror and fascination at the same time.

In Russian folk tales about Ivan, the targets of his anger are usually rich nobles, not the poor. He is shown as smart enough to see through appearances, spotting the worth of a poor man and rewarding him while knocking a proud boyar down a peg or two. And people's imaginations were captured by stories of the wickedly clever tyrant who came up with darkly comic punishments that fit the crime. It was said that an official who had accepted a bribe hidden in a goose was cut and sewn up like a bird for the oven. When a diplomat refused to remove his hat before the czar, Ivan had it nailed to his head.

But pleasing Ivan could be dangerous too, according to legend. He was said to have been very happy with the architect who built St. Basil's Cathedral in Moscow. So pleased, in fact, that he blinded the man—to make sure he could never build another like it anywhere else.

St. Basil's Cathedral in Moscow, built to celebrate Ivan's victory at Kazan.

By 1570, the atmosphere inside Moscow's *oprichniki* court had changed. Passing through its gate, over which a black double-headed eagle scowled, visitors felt the depressed mood that hung in the air. Faces were scared, eyes downcast. The whole place seemed frozen in inaction, with each person wrapped up in fear for his own life.

The *oprichniki* themselves had become the victims of arrests and executions. No longer trusting his body-guards, Ivan purged traitors from his entourage several times. But the czar was still not at ease. His suspicions always fell on whoever had recently been closest to him.

To Ivan, any wavering in obedience was treason. And he had reason to fear treason more than ever. His men abused their powers. Setting off on horseback, they raided homes and stole whatever they liked, loading their sleighs with loot and spreading terror throughout Russia. Robbers took advantage of the people's fear by dressing up as *oprichniki* to carry out their own crimes. No one dared to oppose them or complain.

Ivan became so afraid of his own subjects that he tried twice to secure a safe haven in England—the only country with which he had remained friendly. He even proposed marriage to one of Queen Elizabeth's relatives, Mary Hastings, hoping to bind himself more closely to the English. Elizabeth replied tactfully that Mary was too ill to accept. In the years leading up to this proposal, Ivan's personal life had become chaotic. He had remarried several times, sometimes choosing a bride from a parade of girls he ordered to be arranged before him. Some of these wives died; others Ivan rejected and sent to convents.

The disorder created by Ivan's campaigns of terror had made his old enemies the Tatars bold. In 1571 they attacked Moscow, sacking and burning the city. The following year, just as abruptly as he had created it, Ivan disbanded the *oprichniki*. Even saying the word now became a crime. Some hoped this meant a return to peace and an end to injustice, but they were soon disappointed. Arrests of Ivan's enemies continued, and they were tortured and sentenced without trials, as they had been in the past. Only the titles of Ivan's henchmen had changed.

SPLENDOR AND CRUELTY: EYEWITNESS ACCOUNTS

English envoys were dazzled by the displays of wealth and power in Ivan's court, which they found more splendid than those of the English and French kings. Richard Chancellor noted the hundred courtiers "all appareled in cloth of gold down to their ankles ... Our men began to wonder at the majesty of the emperor. His seat was aloft in a very royal throne, having on his head a crown of gold, appareled with a robe all of goldsmith's work, and in his hand he held a scepter garnished ... with precious stones."

Another guest at Ivan's court was a German adventurer named Heinrich Von Staden, who stayed on to join the *oprichniki*. Von Staden wrote with amazement about the czar who "plundered his own towns and people," along with his henchmen. "The *oprichniki* caused great misery in the country, and many people were secretly murdered," Von Staden wrote. "The *oprichniki* ransacked the entire countryside and all the cities and villages." At the same time, Von Staden was quite willing to help. On one outing, he wrote, "I accompanied [the czar] with one horse ... I finally returned to my estate with 49 horses, 22 pulling sleighs full of goods, which I sent to my house in Moscow."

Finally, after 34 years as czar, Ivan received a blow from which he would never recover. It was a blow he dealt with his own hand.

One day Ivan was exchanging angry words with his eldest son and heir, Czarevich Ivan Ivanovich. In a flash of temper, the czar struck his son with his royal staff. The czarevich died shortly afterwards.

Ivan was horrified by what he had done. He sobbed and tore his hair and beard like a madman. Then he ordered that lists be made of every person he had put to death throughout his reign. It was an enormous task. Secretaries came up with more than 3,000 people, but names could not be found for all of them. Ivan had copies of the lists sent to monasteries, along with tens of thousands of rubles to pay for prayers for the victims' souls. The czar pardoned them all.

Sil'vestr's warnings about a final judgment on his rule had come back to haunt Ivan. What would happen to his own soul? Ivan was tormented by fear. His health was suffering, too. Racked with illness, Ivan asked astrologers to predict his future. Word got back to him that they had also predicted the date of his death— March 18, a day not far off. Ivan was enraged. The astrologers would be burned alive, he said, if they were wrong. It seems not to have occurred to the czar that his order was a strong incentive to carry out his murder.

The 18th of March arrived. Ivan felt well and laughed at the astrologers. He took a bath, and played chess with one of his courtiers. Then, without warning, the czar fainted. There was confusion as courtiers rushed for doctors, a confessor, medicine. Some claimed that Ivan died in the commotion—perhaps not from natural causes. Others said that he took the vows of a monk just before dying.

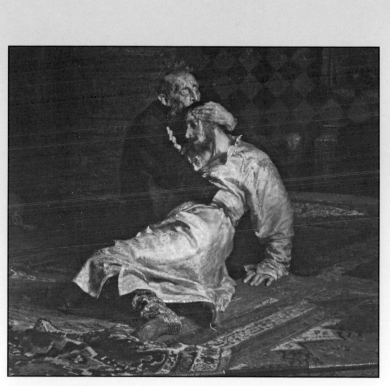

After killing his son in anger, Ivan was haunted by regret. His horror is captured here by a 19th-century Russian artist.

Was Ivan poisoned? One suspect has long been Boris Godunov, a confidant of Ivan's who would himself reign briefly as czar. But this remains a mystery.

Ivan's younger son, the simple-minded Fyodor, could not possibly fill his father's shoes. Amid struggles for power and competing claims for the throne, Russia was invaded by Poland's armies. Ivan's campaigns of terror had left large areas deserted and much of the country in disorder. But the model of the all-powerful czar that he had created would leave a lasting mark. It would continue with Michael Romanov—Anastasiya's grandnephew—who was elected czar by the boyars in 1613, and last until the Romanov czars were toppled by the Russian Revolution in 1917.

ROBESPIERRE
THE REPUBLIC OF VIRTUE

Paris, 1794

Through the Police Bureau's half-open window, the distant whirr of the guillotine and the thud of its falling blade could barely be heard. Much clearer was the roar of the crowd that followed, a sound that rose and fell every few minutes. The string of noises repeated itself as executions proceeded at a steady pace.

Terror is merely prompt, severe, and inflexible justice.
—Maximilien Robespierre

A man sat alone at the desk near the window, hoping a breeze would relieve the summer heat. He was in his mid-thirties, and his dark-colored suit was neat, if a little worn out. Ignoring the shouts of the crowd outside, he adjusted his round spectacles and smoothed his hair.

The man eyed the stack of papers on his tidy desk. They were newly arrived reports sent by informers from across France. The letters contained the names of "counter-revolutionaries," people whose suspicious actions had been noted by government agents or zealous citizens. A former aristocrat was accused of "dangerous excesses." A patriotic club asked that priests be forced to report to authorities daily, as nobles did. The man frowned as he read the second letter, and he scribbled an order for an agent to check out this so-called patriotic club. What were they really up to? Informants themselves were often worthy objects of suspicion.

The roar of the crowd peaked for an instant, and the man glanced up. But he soon returned to his note-taking, penning his name on an arrest warrant for the ex-aristocrat, ignoring the noise of the sinister machine he had set in motion.

For just a single year, this man—Maximilien Robespierre— would be the most powerful person in France. He was not a king, but an ordinary citizen swept to power by the people. For a brief time he would hold the police, the courts, the government, and the people themselves in his hands. For in what other hands would they be safe? As Robespierre said himself, he was the defender of the Revolution and the voice of the people. He was also the chief architect of a reign of terror that would claim at least 35,000 lives before it ended.

As a boy in small-town France, Maximilien had never dreamed of how the country would change in his lifetime, or that he would ever attain the power he did. An absolute monarch reigned over France, and the country's riches and privileges were reserved for a small group of aristocrats. While the luxury of the French royal court was legendary, millions of French lived in squalid poverty. The regime's lavish spending, wars, and heavy taxes on the people had made it more and more unpopular. Its downfall was on the way.

Few could see that downfall coming in 1775, least of all Maximilien. That year the 17-year-old was chosen from among all the boys of his school to deliver a short speech in Latin to the new king. Louis XVI and his wife, Marie Antoinette, would pass by the school on their way home from the coronation ceremony.

Maximilien was at his Paris school, Louis-le-Grand, thanks to a scholarship he had won when he was 11. His family could never have afforded it otherwise. In his hometown of Arras, Maximilien had lived happily until his mother died in childbirth when he was six. Two years later his father abandoned the four children, who were divided among relatives. Maximilien, the oldest, went to live with his aunts. His sister Charlotte noticed a dramatic change in her brother: the once cheerful boy became unsmiling and now took his responsibilities very seriously. When his younger brother and sisters played, he looked on solemnly, more likely to enforce the rules of the game than to join in.

At school, Robespierre worked hard—never a brilliant student, but determined. He had such a knack for Latin that he was nicknamed "the Roman," and it was this talent that had won him the chance to read before the king. To the other boys he seemed quiet, never laughing or mixing easily. He was, after all, a poor boy in a famous school full of rich children. Louis-le-Grand was known for being liberal and open-minded; new ideas about equality and freedom were often discussed. But the line between scholarship boys and the sons of dukes and government ministers remained.

Maximilien had scrounged money for a new suit and a pair of shoes to wear for his speech. Flanked by the head teachers, he stood stiffly outside the school as the king's carriage approached. He was nervous, his throat dry. On cue, Maximilien began his address, straining to make his thin, high-pitched voice carry. But in a few moments it was all over. The royal carriage pulled away over the gravel driveway. The king had not even bothered to get out.

Robespierre stayed at Louis-le-Grand until he was a young man of 22, leaving in 1780 with a law degree and a prize for good conduct. He moved back to Arras, where he set out to make a name for himself as a defense lawyer.

At home with his sister, his life was simple and disciplined. You could set a clock by Robespierre's daily routine of plain meals, work, and an evening walk.

ROBESPIERRE: FACTS

Born: May 6, 1758
Died: July 28, 1794
Name at birth: Maximilien-François-Marie-Isidore de Robespierre
Titles in power: Various, including Member of Committee of Public Safety, President of the National Convention
Age upon coming to power: 35
Time in power: 1 year
Size of domain: France, approx. 547,000 sq km (210,000 square miles)
Armed forces commanded: Revolutionary armies, over 980,000 men, as well as France's police
Number of victims: 35,000–40,000 (16,594 sentenced to death during the terror, over 10,000 died in prison, and over 10,000 executed without trial)
Defining characteristics: idealistic, unwilling to compromise, ruthless
Legacy: Preached ideals, such as equality and liberty, that have had a lasting influence. Some historians believe Robespierre's revolutionary government provided the model for the dictatorships of the 20th century.

Around young women he was formal and awkward. He did not care for luxuries, but he was careful, almost finicky, about his appearance. His clothes and powdered hair were always neat and proper. The shabbily dressed Louis-le-Grand student was gone for good; the new Robespierre was determined to fit in and succeed.

He was also determined to make the most of his legal cases. In one of these, Robespierre defended a local man who had installed a lightning rod, a new invention. The man's neighbor feared it would draw lightning to his own house and demanded that it be removed. As usual, Robespierre did not worry about the legal details. Something larger was at stake here, he argued in the important tone that was becoming familiar to the judges of Arras. It was a clear battle between science and superstition. His client was like many great minds of the past—Galileo, for instance—persecuted and misunderstood.

Like most of Robespierre's clients, the man with the lightning rod couldn't afford to pay him much. But that was not important to the young lawyer. He jumped at cases involving big issues, especially injustice and human rights. Since his student days, Robespierre had adored the books of Jean-Jacques Rousseau, who declared that government should reflect the general will of the people. These ideas struck Robespierre so powerfully that he began to think of himself as Rousseau's disciple, putting the writer's words into action.

In his hands, another case turned into a crusade for the working class, with Robespierre lashing out against the clergy and the court itself. But this time the judge gave him a stern warning: in criticizing the Church and the court, Robespierre had gone too far.

The judge's words were still ringing in his ears as Robespierre packed up his papers in the emptying courtroom. Inside, he was stewing. Despite his successes, he'd been getting fewer cases lately. He knew he had come as far as he could within a regime that recognized only those who had friends and family in high places.

Frustrated, he had already published some of his ideas in pamphlets. They showed the seeds of notions that would grow into obsessions in the stormy years to come. Others were plotting against him, he wrote, hampering his career. Hidden enemies threatened not only himself but the nation.

INSPIRING A REVOLUTION

Like many revolutionaries, Robespierre admired the writings of the social philosopher Jean-Jacques Rousseau. Human beings are naturally good, Rousseau argued, but society corrupts them. What was needed was a government that expressed the "general will" of the people. This will was always right. Robespierre wanted the French Revolution to be a pure example of Rousseau's teachings. There was no room for compromise.

He also took some of Rousseau's ideas to dangerous conclusions. "The people always wants the good but it does not always recognize it," Rousseau wrote. Robespierre understood this to mean that the public may not know what is good for them. It was up to someone like him—a "pure" patriot—to tell them.

Robespierre never stopped praising "the people," even while sending many of them to the guillotine. He saw no contradiction: "The people is sublime," he declared, "but individuals are weak." Over time his notion of who "the people" were got narrower, as he excluded more and more "traitors" from his definition: those who were lukewarm about the Revolution, those who rioted for food, those who disagreed with him, anyone whose record was "impure." In the end, there remained only himself.

In 1789 came a once-in-a-lifetime chance, an opportunity to leapfrog out of his stalled career. Robespierre seized it. The Estates General, a council made up of France's three estates—nobles, clergy, and commoners—was set to meet at the king's palace in Versailles in May. No king had called a meeting of this council for 175 years. Now it would gather to deal with the huge debts overwhelming the country. Robespierre was determined to be one of the five delegates from his province, and he campaigned hard to get elected.

Maximilien Robespierre arrived at Versailles, just outside Paris, an unknown young man with two black suits. He knew there was only one way to make a name for himself among the throng of deputies: despite terrible stage fright, he forced himself to step up to the speaker's podium. He was not a natural at public speaking. He read most of his speech, making fussy gestures with his hands. His accent betrayed that he came from the countryside. Sometimes he was heckled, but this did not stop him from going back to the podium again and again—demanding that slaves in France's colonies be freed, defending the freedom of the press, urging that the king's powers be limited.

A more experienced delegate, the Count of Mirabeau, recognized at once that Robespierre's earnest enthusiasm was bound to win him support. "He'll go far," Mirabeau told a friend. "He believes everything he says."

Once underway, the Estates General turned out to be much more than a debate about France's financial woes. Members from the third estate—the commoners—were joined by some idealistic nobles and clergy in demanding that changes be made to the unfair regime. First of all, they insisted that the commons, which represented over 90 percent of the population, should have more say in decisions. No one could have predicted how fast that change would come, and many were caught up by the exhilarating speed at which events began to unfold.

In June, the third estate deputies defiantly renamed themselves the National Assembly, since they were the genuine representatives of the people. Locked out of the council's meeting room, members of the National Assembly took a dramatic oath not to break up until a new constitution was passed to right the wrongs of the monarchy. Meanwhile, in the streets of Paris, violent outbursts showed that ordinary people were hungry for change, too. A month later, the Bastille, France's most notorious prison, was stormed by a mob of Parisians. What had begun as a movement for reform had turned into a revolution.

Much more confident now as a deputy, Robespierre felt a personal duty to direct the tide of these events. There may have been some sighs as the now familiar figure stepped up again to the podium of the National Assembly. Looking slim and pale behind the lectern, Robespierre pushed his round steel-rimmed glasses onto his forehead. When he began to speak, his tone was flat yet oddly threatening.

As usual, Robespierre was indignant about something. This time his outrage was aimed at the death penalty. Death sentences were "solemn crimes," he declared, "committed … not by individuals but by the nation at large." Cruel laws, the work of tyrants, were the chains that bound the human race.

Earlier, Robespierre had raged against granting the

vote only to landowners. To many Assembly members, this new law seemed better than the people having no vote at all; it was at least a step in the direction of equal rights. While few disagreed with Robespierre's ideals, they simply expected change to come more slowly. But Robespierre refused to accept compromise in any form. "If you do not do everything for liberty, you will have done nothing," he declared. "There are not two ways of being free: one must be so entirely or one becomes once more a slave."

Good and evil were at odds on these issues, he insisted, and there was only one right answer. By now Robespierre had begun to make the Revolution a personal crusade. It was he who stood for what was right, who spoke the people's will. Liberty and truth were always attacked by enemies, he declared, but he was not afraid to die for his beliefs.

Some of the deputies snickered at this, but their laughter would soon grow uneasy. As public support for Robespierre continued to mount, the snickering would stop altogether. Robespierre was already popular with the city workers and revolutionaries outside the Assembly. They read his speeches once they were printed and circulated. His refusal to compromise earned their respect, and they dubbed him "the Incorruptible."

Robespierre often delivered the same words to the Jacobins, a political club where he felt much more at home. Nicknamed for the old Jacobin monastery where its members met, the club was an informal gathering of like-minded deputies. The Jacobins were radical and eager to speed up the pace of change. Among them Robespierre faced no hecklers; he was more likely to be greeted with a standing ovation from men with tears in their eyes. Robespierre had learned quickly the importance of political clubs, whose members could control the direction of the Assembly by meeting beforehand to plan ways to influence it.

Robespierre's idealism reached its height in May 1791. The delegates had completed their task—drafting a new constitution. Soon they would be replaced by a new government body, the Legislative Assembly. Robespierre now shocked the other deputies by making a bold motion. No one in the current assembly should be

Robespierre believed violence would drive the Revolution forward. On July 13, 1789, riots spread through Paris when the price of grain went up, and workers looted buildings for food and weapons. Here the Maison de St-Lazare, a prison run by priests, is attacked.

THE FRENCH REVOLUTION: A TIMELINE

1789

King Louis XVI, an absolute monarch, rules France.

May: Financial troubles force the king to open the Estates General.

June: The third estate renames itself the National Assembly. Many nobles and clergy join them.

July: Parisians storm the Bastille. Popular revolts continue through the summer.

August: The National Assembly abolishes the privileges of nobles and proclaims the Declaration of the Rights of Man and the Citizen.

1791

June: The royal family tries to escape, but they are caught and returned to Paris.

July: The National Guard fires on crowds petitioning to establish a republic.

September: The Assembly completes a new constitution. Louis promises to uphold it.

October: The new Legislative Assembly begins.

1792

January–March: Parisians riot over food shortages. A backlash against the Revolution begins in parts of France.

April: France goes to war against Austria.

June: Mobs storm the king's Tuileries Palace.

July: The Legislative Assembly grants the government emergency powers. Most of Europe is allied against revolutionary France.

September: The first meeting of the National Convention. Members abolish the monarchy and declare France a republic.

1793

January: King Louis is executed.

February: France goes to war against Britain, Holland, and Spain. Civil war continues in parts of France opposed to the Revolution.

March: The Revolutionary Tribunal is established.

April: The Committee of Public Safety is formed by the Convention. The Reign of Terror begins.

September–October: The Convention suspends the new constitution. The government lies in the hands of the Committee of Public Safety.

November: Decrees against priests and religious beliefs are passed.

1794

June: The Law of 22 Prairial removes the rights of the accused before the Revolutionary Tribunal.

July: Robespierre is arrested and executed. The powers of the Revolutionary Tribunal are curbed.

1799

The military leader Napoleon Bonaparte takes over the government in a coup. He becomes First Consul for Life, then Emperor.

elected to the next, he declared from the podium. The new assembly should start with a clean slate, without any trace of the old regime. Sacrifice yourselves for the good of the Revolution, he urged the deputies. He would do the same, barring himself from playing any role in the new government.

One deputy spoke up. Why must they start all over? Did Robespierre believe the Revolution should go on forever? Did he want to invite a possible dictatorship? Robespierre remained silent, and his motion was carried.

When he stepped out into the street on the last day of the National Assembly, Robespierre was mobbed by a cheering crowd. Someone offered him a baby to hold. Moments later he was carried triumphantly on the people's shoulders. On his way home to Arras, his carriage was mobbed again as crowds showered it with flower petals.

King Louis XVI shocked the country when, in June 1791, he and the royal family tried to escape Paris. They were alarmed by the Paris mobs, who were no longer afraid to show their hostility to the monarchy. But Louis and his family were caught and taken into the custody of the new government.

A month later, several thousand petitioners gathered one morning in Paris's Champ de Mars, an old military exercise grounds. They declared that the king had abdicated his throne when he fled and should be kept from returning to it. A republic was what France needed, the petitioners urged. They attracted many supporters. By the afternoon, 50,000 people thronged the square. The mayor of Paris sent in the National Guard. When the crowd began throwing stones, the

National Guard troops, led by the Marquis de Lafayette, open fire upon the crowd gathered at the Champ de Mars in 1791. The incident drew a line between revolutionaries who wanted moderate change and those who wanted to overthrow the king.

guards opened fire, killing 50 people and scattering the terrified crowd.

In the wake of the demonstration, radical revolutionaries feared they might be arrested, or worse, and Robespierre was afraid to continue staying at the Paris room he rented. A carpenter named Maurice Duplay, one of the growing number of Robespierre's admirers, offered his home as a refuge. Robespierre agreed to spend the night for safety's sake, but he ended up moving in for good.

The Duplay home was a short walk from the Jacobin Club, and there Robespierre felt safe and close to supporters. Duplay's wife and daughters were thrilled with their heroic guest, and they flattered and pampered him. After working in his small room overlooking the timber yard, Robespierre would come out to find coffee ready and the table laid with a bowl of oranges, his favorite food. Care was taken to plan meals and daily life around Robespierre's work, and his portrait hung on several walls. Soon Robespierre was too comfortable to leave this pleasant cocoon. He enjoyed reading plays to the Duplay girls in the evening, but he scoffed when a friend hinted that Robespierre might marry one of them. He would never marry, Robespierre responded firmly—his life was the Revolution.

Some of his colleagues grumbled about his new living arrangements. In his cheap flat, Robespierre had been available to friends and patriots. But Jacobins who tried to visit him now were barred by Madame Duplay, who jealously guarded Robespierre's privacy.

Robespierre may have shut himself out of the new Legislative Assembly, but thanks to his growing reputation he was offered a plum job as attorney-general of a new court, the Supreme Criminal Tribunal. Like several other revolutionaries, Robespierre also started his own newspaper, *The Defender of the Constitution*, to spread his views now that the speaker's podium was off limits.

Robespierre had not been at the Champ de Mars demonstration, but that did not stop him writing a dramatic account of it afterwards. Neither had he seen the fall of the Bastille with his own eyes. He was also at home with the Duplays when, in August 1792, a mob of armed citizens stormed the king's Tuileries Palace, overthrowing the monarchy. Violent uprisings were needed for the triumph of liberty over tyranny, Robespierre often wrote, but he never took part in them. He had a genius for describing the events once they were over, explaining their importance to the Revolution. The heroes of his stories were always "the people." In their faces shone the love of liberty. But Robespierre played down the brutality of these events. Behind vague words, he disguised the massacre of hundreds of royal guards who had surrendered to the mob at the Tuileries.

Robespierre's star continued to rise. After the August revolt he was elected to the Commune of Paris, the city's new revolutionary government, which spoke for Paris's workers and tradespeople. Its members had masterminded the assault on the Tuileries. In a sign of things to come, the Commune installed a recent invention in Paris's main square. Called a guillotine, the new machine was designed to make executions painless with a falling blade that quickly separated head from body.

All this time Robespierre had one pressing issue in mind: who would be elected to the National Convention? The Legislative Assembly had called countrywide elections to form this governing body, which would replace the two assemblies. Robespierre had no intention of barring himself as a candidate this time. He used his position in the Commune to spread the word to voters. Only patriots must be elected, he insisted, meaning himself and his fellow Jacobins. The voters agreed. All 24 Paris representatives elected to the Convention were Robespierre's political allies. The first Paris deputy to win a seat was Robespierre himself.

What to do with King Louis—that was the question troubling the National Convention. The new government was more radical than either of the assemblies that had come before it. Gone now was any voice from the nobles; poor and middle-class members held all the seats. The Convention abolished the monarchy and declared France a republic. All the titles of the old regime—*roi, seigneur*, even *monsieur* and *madame*—were outlawed. From now on every man and woman would simply be "citizen."

Some wanted to spare the former king, now Citizen Louis Capet, destroying only his royal title and position. But to Robespierre, any weakness shown over the king would be fatal to the new republic. As an elected

Revolutionaries execute King Louis XVI in 1793. The Reign of Terror that followed would send thousands more to the guillotine.

member of the new Convention, he was back at the speaker's tribune, using it to teach others their duty. There could be no question of a trial, he argued. It would be a step backwards; it would be putting the Revolution itself on trial. The people had judged the king when they stormed the Tuileries.

What of Robespierre's earlier fight against the death penalty? He had answers for anyone who might wonder at this about-face. "Yes, the death penalty in general is a crime," he admitted. But this case was special. The people's liberty was still young and vulnerable, he said. A death sentence for the king was needed to protect the new republic. The Convention must be careful not to confuse laws meant for individuals with actions needed to safeguard a nation. "Louis must die in order that our country may live," he urged. "I demand that he be made a great example of before the whole world."

The trial of the king went ahead, and Louis was convicted of crimes such as "conspiring against liberty." Unlike the crowds who filled the streets, Robespierre did not watch the king's trip by cart to the guillotine. He remained indoors, working. There was much to be done; this execution was only the beginning. France was at war with the monarchies of Europe, who were hostile to the Revolution. Even more dangerous, in Robespierre's mind, were the enemies within. Countless traitors to the republic must be exposed and destroyed. But first, the arguments in the Convention—where moderate and extremist members often disagreed—had to be stopped. "What is needed," he jotted in his notebook, "is a single will."

Some Convention members—deputies known as Girondins, who had tried to save the king—attacked Robespierre. He was creating a dictatorship for himself, they cried, and the Paris Commune was too powerful. But Robespierre defended himself at the speaker's tribune. Harshness was needed to sustain the Revolution, he declared. If you condemned violent measures, you condemned the Revolution itself. His pronouncements were met with thunderous applause. The Girondins were silenced. Within a few months they would be expelled from the Convention; within a year they would all be executed.

Robespierre's speeches to the Convention had taken on a darker hue. To the noble ideals of the Revolution—liberty, equality, and virtue—he now added more sinister themes. Traitors were everywhere. Worse, they were hard to see. They looked like patriots, talked like patriots, but in their hearts they wanted to turn back the clock and destroy the republic. The only defense was to be ruthless in weeding them out.

See to it that the blade of the law moves horizontally, so as to strike off all the heads of the great conspirators.
—Robespierre

Many revolutionaries agreed that the new republic was in danger. The armies of England, Prussia, Austria, Holland, and Spain were pushing against France's borders and blocking its ports. Inside France, food shortages were causing widespread hunger and riots. The republic could be toppled before it had truly begun. Until the danger passed, extraordinary measures were needed.

Robespierre called for a new kind of court, one that could punish political crimes without the delays of trials that relied on evidence and proof of guilt. As long as the judges were true patriots, he said, they would reach the right verdict quickly.

In March 1793, the Revolutionary Tribunal was created for "counter-revolutionary crimes." There would be no appealing its decisions, and sentences would be carried out within 24 hours. Robespierre himself drafted the list of candidates virtuous enough to sit in judgment. To him, their ability mattered much less than their patriotism. He kept running lists of patriots whose revolutionary virtues could be depended upon, noting if they were "honest," "enlightened," and, most important, "pure."

In July, Robespierre was handed more power when the Convention elected him to the Committee of Public Safety, a group of 12 who met in secret to decide what laws and measures were needed to defend the republic. No records were kept of their meetings around a long green table in a room in the old Tuileries Palace, but their votes determined the fate of many thousands. In this time of crisis, Robespierre explained, the Committee would "crush rebels and intimidate conspirators." Although the Committee had no official chief, Robespierre was the undisputed leader.

To keep an eye on France's armies and control the population outside Paris, Robespierre relied on allies he could trust—especially his younger brother, Augustin, and Louis Antoine de Saint-Just, a keen young admirer of Robespierre. Committees were set up around the country to spy on citizens and submit regular lists of suspects: people who looked like "enemies of liberty" or "supporters of tyranny"; those without jobs; anyone who had been out of the country during the Revolution; former nobles and their relatives. All the machinery for a reign of terror had been put in place. It had only to be set in motion.

In the room where the Paris parliament used to meet, a grim ritual was underway. The king's throne and the sumptuous royal tapestries were gone, long wooden tables and platforms having taken their place. The Revolutionary Tribunal was in session.

Heroes of the early Revolution were now being branded "counter-revolutionaries" because they were not zealous enough. One condemned man wrote to his wife that he was on his way to die because "what was a virtue yesterday is a crime today." Robespierre's suspicious glance had even come to rest on the man he had replaced on the Committee of Public Safety: Georges-Jacques Danton.

Danton, a popular revolutionary, had started calling for a slowdown of the executions. The danger was past, he argued. Sometimes vulgar, always outspoken, Danton had also made the mistake of mocking Robespierre's ideas about a republic inspired by virtue. Robespierre signed the warrant for Danton's arrest as well as those of Danton's known associates. Among them was Camille Desmoulins, one of Robespierre's only boyhood friends at Louis-le-Grand. Desmoulins's newspaper had called for a halt to the terror and defended freedom of the press.

As he was brought to stand before the judges' wooden table, Danton knew he was already condemned. But it was his last chance to appeal to the crowds who were packed along the sides and in the doorways of the room. When the time came to present his defense, his booming voice could be heard even in the streets below the court. Danton spoke well, and the judges could see that the spectators were taking his side. One nervous judge quickly passed a note down the table, and the judges announced that the trial had been postponed.

LEVERS OF POWER

Like a man pulling many levers to control a complex machine, Robespierre wielded power through a number of organizations. Together, they made him the most powerful person in the country.

National Convention: The revolutionary government, to which Robespierre was elected a Paris deputy and where he briefly served as its president. Here he made his influential speeches.

Jacobin Club: Robespierre used this political club to influence votes in the National Convention. He made sure his Jacobin allies were in all the key government positions.

Committee of Public Safety: The National Convention gave this small group the power to undertake "all measures necessary for the internal and external defense of the Republic." Robespierre was responsible for political justice and police, policy, and ideology. The committee's powers, and Robespierre's, were greatly increased by France's war against Europe's monarchies, and the CPS became a dictatorship. It ran the government and the war, and it had the power to issue arrest warrants.

Revolutionary Tribunal: The special court for counter-revolutionary crimes. Robespierre controlled who its judges were and sent anyone he suspected of treason to appear before it.

Police Bureau: A general police bureau was put under the control of the Committee of Public Safety in April 1794, giving the Committee and Robespierre policing powers.

While in name Robespierre shared power with others—especially the other 11 members of the Committee of Public Safety—he was the linchpin that connected them all.

When the Tribunal reopened, Danton was told that no more testimony would be heard. The trial was closed. "Closed?" he thundered. "Why, it has not begun! You haven't read the evidence, you haven't heard the witnesses!" At Danton's side, Desmoulins crumpled up the words he had written in his own defense and threw them to the ground.

Desmoulins's wife fled the courtroom and hurried to Robespierre. She begged him to spare the life of his old friend. Robespierre showed no sign of being moved. As the cart carrying the condemned men rolled over the cobblestones towards the guillotine, Danton shouted a bold prediction: Robespierre would shortly be following them.

On a sunny June day in 1794, Robespierre felt as if a dream had come true. A landslide majority vote had made him the new president of the National Convention. And as president he was presiding over the Festival of the Supreme Being—the beginning of a new state religion for France.

Robespierre had always fought against those who wanted to destroy religion along with the monarchy. Many revolutionaries had attacked the Church for being part of the old regime, and Notre-Dame Cathedral in Paris had even been renamed the Temple of Reason. But although Robespierre no longer considered himself a Christian, he still believed in God. The people also needed to believe in a higher power to inspire them to virtue, he argued. So today was a triumph for him.

Dressed for the occasion in a blue coat, tricolor sash, and plumed hat, Robespierre opened with a speech in the Tuileries Gardens. A procession to the Champ de

Mars followed, where almost the entire population of Paris gathered to watch. But there were sarcastic whispers among the Convention members during the ceremony, some of them reaching Robespierre's ears. "There's the dictator!" one man was reported to have sneered. "It's not enough to be king! He wants to be God!" Rumors had already spread outside France that Robespierre was planning to replace the emergency government with a personal rule. In the end, the new religion turned out to be a mistake. Revolutionary atheists were offended and so were devout Catholics.

Robespierre was at the height of his power. Yet, like a man standing on a cliff edge, he was poised for a fall. The police, the courts, and the government were either under his control or in the hands of his allies. But in his speeches he called himself the victim of traitors, a lone defender of virtue in a universe filled with hidden enemies.

Robespierre's belief that he was destined for a martyr's death was confirmed one day when a girl was found in the Duplays' timber yard under his window. She had a knife with her. "I wanted to see what a tyrant looked like," she replied simply when asked what she was doing there. Assassin or not, the girl was guillotined. "Liberty is exposed to new dangers!" Robespierre wrote in a hysterical letter to his loyal follower Saint-Just.

Soon after the Festival, Robespierre and his Committee passed a new law that would make the Revolutionary Tribunal more powerful and dangerous than ever. Suspects could no longer have a defense lawyer or call witnesses. Proof of guilt would no longer be needed; the word of a patriotic witness was enough. The judges would have to choose between only two verdicts—acquittal or death.

FRANCE AT THE TIME OF THE REVOLUTION

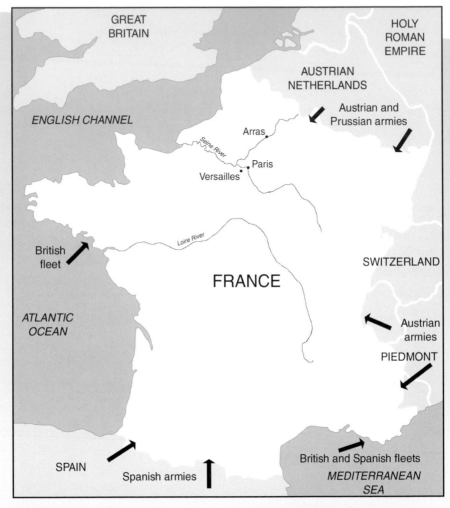

GREAT BRITAIN

HOLY ROMAN EMPIRE

AUSTRIAN NETHERLANDS

Austrian and Prussian armies

ENGLISH CHANNEL

Arras

Seine River

Paris

Versailles

British fleet

Loire River

SWITZERLAND

FRANCE

Austrian armies

PIEDMONT

ATLANTIC OCEAN

SPAIN

Spanish armies

British and Spanish fleets

MEDITERRANEAN SEA

➤ Arrows indicate attacks against revolutionary France by European countries.

Having overthrown its king, France was soon menaced by the monarchies of Europe, which felt threatened by the new republic. Many revolutionaries welcomed war as a chance to spread the Revolution abroad—with the exception of Robespierre. He distrusted France's generals and feared putting the new republic into the hands of men who might betray it and set up a military dictatorship. It was one of the only debates Robespierre lost, and war was declared on Austria in 1792.

Some had hoped the revolutionary government would disappear when France's crises—the war, the food shortages—were under control and democracy was in place. But now it looked as if it was here to stay. Paris prisons were overflowing with thousands of suspects. However, the new law quickly emptied them. That June and July, more people would die on the guillotine than had been executed since the Revolutionary Tribunal began. And yet the man who controlled the machine believed himself to be alone and persecuted.

Robespierre and his allies had met resistance in both the Convention and the Committee over the new laws curbing the rights of suspects. So Robespierre stopped attending both bodies to concentrate on running his Police Bureau. But he could not shake the belief that he was surrounded by traitors, and he could stand it no longer: he must strike first. In July 1794, after six weeks' absence, he returned to the National Convention and stepped up to the tribune.

I am the people myself!
—Robespierre

For two hours he spoke, defending himself against the charges made behind his back. He was no dictator, he said, but a martyr to the republic, a slave of freedom. "They call me a tyrant," he declared. "One arrives at a tyrant's throne by the help of scoundrels. What faction do I belong to? You yourselves."

There was a conspiracy within the Convention, he continued, a plot against him and against the republic. To Robespierre, they had become one and the same. "Make a clean sweep," he pronounced. The Convention must purge the committees, unify the government under one authority. "How can anyone reproach a man who has truth on his side and who knows how to die for his country?" he concluded dramatically.

Robespierre looked out across the crowded Convention room. He waited for someone to speak out, to denounce the traitors by name now that he had pointed the way. The Convention would then vote for their arrest, he believed. But this did not happen. Instead, an argument followed. In the midst of it, one deputy stood up and shouted, "It is time to tell the whole truth. One man is paralyzing the National Convention. That man is the one who has just made the speech. It is Robespierre." The delegates reeled with shock, and all eyes focused on Robespierre.

Taken by surprise, Robespierre felt his mind go blank. He had no clever response, and the other Convention members noticed this show of weakness. Robespierre could not see it yet, but he had made a fatal mistake. By denouncing "traitors" without naming names, he had frightened most of the Convention. Any one of them could be the terror's next victim.

By the time the Convention met again the next day, Robespierre's enemies—until now scattered and fighting among themselves— were united in their purpose: not to let Robespierre or any of his allies speak. When Saint-Just stepped up to the podium, he was interrupted by one deputy after another.

Fear for their lives made Robespierre's opponents bold. One of them, nodding towards Robespierre, was particularly daring: "He says, 'So-and-so conspires against me. I am the friend of the republic. Therefore he conspires against the republic.' This logic is new." Robespierre rose to answer but was greeted by shouts. A wave of protest began to overwhelm him. The tide of the Convention had turned.

When Robespierre next opened his mouth to speak, his throat tightened. He sputtered and lost his voice.

"Danton's blood is choking him!" someone cried.

Robespierre recovered his voice at last. "Cowards!" he spat out. "So you want to avenge Danton? Why, then, did you not defend him?"

"Arrest him!" an almost unknown deputy shouted. A hasty vote was passed to arrest Robespierre along with his allies, including his brother and Saint-Just. Stunned by what had happened, Robespierre at first refused to budge. Finally the men, five in all, were escorted out of the Convention under guard.

The prisons of Paris were loyal to the Commune, still a bastion of support for Robespierre. The jailers refused to hold the arrested men. Robespierre and his friends fled to the Commune headquarters. That night, the Convention declared them outlaws. Now they had only to be identified to be executed; no trial was needed.

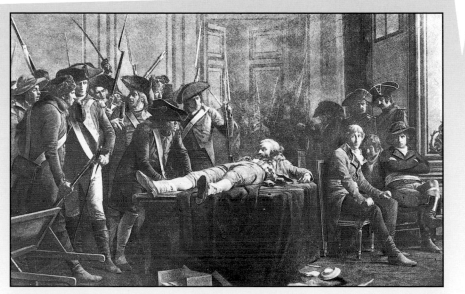

The arrested Robespierre lies wounded on a table on the morning of July 28, 1794.

As the Convention mustered its troops, the outlawed men scrambled to gather supporters. "We must write to the armies," one of Robespierre's followers suggested. But under what authority could they issue the order? "We shall write in the name of the French people," Robespierre declared at last.

Troops from the Convention burst through the door moments later. Robespierre's jaw was shattered by a gunshot. Was it an attack by the invading troops or a suicide attempt? Witnesses would later disagree over what had happened.

Troops carried the wounded Robespierre on a plank through the streets. In the waiting room of the Committee of Public Safety, he was laid on a table. A man standing nearby searched for some cloth to stanch the bleeding. Finding none, he offered Robespierre a piece of paper. "Merci, monsieur," Robespierre murmured. Bystanders exchanged glances: he had used the polite "monsieur" from the old regime, not the revolutionary "citizen." Traditional manners died hard in the graduate of Louis-le-Grand.

Within hours, a bandaged Robespierre was riding in a cart to the guillotine at the Place de la Révolution, where a boisterous crowd waited. Unlike many other victims of the terror, he uttered no memorable last words. Only a scream escaped his mouth when the executioner removed the bandage from his jaw to expose his neck.

The five-man Directory that next governed France took a moderate direction. But in 1799, a coup backed by France's military overthrew the Directory. France returned to one-man rule under the military commander Napoleon Bonaparte, who crowned himself emperor in 1804.

HITLER
ONE PEOPLE,
ONE REICH,
ONE FÜHRER

Germany, 1934

An immense procession wound its way through the dusk. The tramp of marching boots echoed on the stone streets of Nuremberg. On either side, huge but orderly crowds pressed in. Some marchers held red-and-black flags, others carried poles topped with gold eagles. All wore the same brown uniforms with red arm bands.

That you have found me ... among so many millions is the miracle of our time! And that I have found you, that is Germany's fortune!
—Adolf Hitler

The parade reached its destination: the foot of a massive platform. Above it towered a giant spotlit eagle, its wings stretching over 30 meters (100 feet).

The annual rally of the National Socialist German Workers' Party—known as the Nazis—was about to reach a climax. All week the city's medieval buildings had been draped with the party's red-and-black flags, and hundreds of thousands of people had filled the streets. Now the eager crowds were waiting for the high point of the day's events. Their party leader, now chancellor of Germany, would speak.

The crowd parted, and Adolf Hitler, surrounded by his storm troopers, approached the broad stairs of the review stand. As usual, he chose to walk through the people rather than appear from somewhere above them. From time to time he returned their enthusiastic salutes with his own raised right hand, walking briskly in his brown uniform. Hitler believed in surrounding himself with symbols of power, but in the middle of it all he liked to appear modest. A plain man of action. A man of the people.

He stepped up to the speaker's podium and looked out over the sea of 30,000 red flags stretching before him. It was a spectacular effect dreamed up by Hitler's favorite architect, Albert Speer, who shared his love of grand scenes. The crowd was massive—nearly 150,000 uniformed men and another 100,000 spectators—but in perfect order. Everything had been carefully arranged to display power and perfect unity: one people united in a single will under a supreme commander. Like the setting, the hour had been carefully chosen. Night was best for speaking to crowds; minds were easier to influence at the end of the day. Later, eyes would be dazzled when 130 searchlights ringing the field were aimed at the sky, their beams blazing like enormous pillars into the air, circling the assembly in a "cathedral of light."

After a moment of silence Hitler began to speak, slowly at first, in simple, clipped phrases. He often sounded hesitant at the beginning of a speech, warming up only after he had sensed the crowd's mood.

Soon he started to point, stressing words with a jab of his fist. Then his voice grew louder, rising to a higher pitch. Spitting out his words, his left hand clenched at his side, he sliced and punched the air with his right. "It is our people's great misery that moved us, united us in battle, and made us fight and get strong, and all those who have not suffered the same misery among their own people are therefore unable to understand us."

Hitler paused a moment, hands clasped, to receive thunderous applause. His words were not original or deep. But it was not so much what Hitler said as how he said it that stirred up the audience into a frenzy. As the speech built to a climax, his voice became harsher, his gestures more violent. He jerked his head and pounded his chest as he hoarsely shouted out his words. Then, ending abruptly, he turned and left the crowd cheering.

Hitler (on platform) speaks to the massive crowds gathered for the Nazis' annual party rally in Nuremberg. Behind him SA men hold the party's standards.

Not many years before, he had been dismissed as a nobody on the fringes of society, without connections or influence; in his own words, one of the "nameless." Now he was the absolute ruler of over 60 million Germans, and about to lead them down a path to war and destruction. How did this "nobody" come so far so fast?

Nothing about Hitler's early years hinted at such a dramatic climb to the top. He was not even born in Germany, but in a small town in the neighboring German-speaking country of Austria. Hitler's father was a customs official who had worked hard to get his modest job and expected Adolf to do the same. He was also a stern and brutal man. Hitler's mother, much younger than his father, smothered her son with affection and tenderness, as if to make up for the beatings.

Dreamy and unwilling to work hard, Hitler soon found school painful. The pale, thin boy would much rather be drawing or reading the adventure stories he loved. History class was the exception: Hitler was thrilled by heroic tales from Germany's past. Despite his poor marks, Hitler became convinced by his own knack for drawing that he was destined for a greater career than his father's—as an artist.

When his father took him to visit his customs office, Hitler was horrified by such a dull life. "I yawned and grew sick to my stomach at the thought of sitting in an office," he later recalled. Hitler stubbornly resisted his father's plans for him, and more violent showdowns at home followed.

When Hitler was 13, his father died. Young Adolf convinced his doting mother that he was too ill to keep traveling to his school, an hour away in the town of Linz, and at 16 he dropped out. For two years Hitler lived idly, reading and drawing, while his mother and younger sister cooked and cleaned for him. Sometimes he went to the theater in Linz with his only close friend, a quiet boy named August Kubizek. Adolf daydreamed of the great things he would do but never roused himself to work towards any goal. He was sure he had a great future ahead of him. But what?

At 18, Hitler made up his mind: he would move to Vienna, Austria's capital, and study art. He begged Kubizek, an aspiring musician, to come too. Vienna was a splendid, cosmopolitan city, and young Hitler was in awe of it, especially its Opera House. He and Kubizek would line up for hours to buy cheap tickets that allowed them to stand at the back. Peering over heads, Hitler was soon completely caught up in the performance. He would return many times to see the same show, always an opera by Richard Wagner. Hitler was thrilled by Wagner's heroic world of German myths, where larger-than-life heroes and gods struggled on an epic scale. The operas were filled with darker images too—heroic deaths, a world destroyed in flames.

After the show, Hitler, his face radiant, would talk excitedly to his one-person audience—about art, society, the world. Kubizek, shy and naive, was very receptive to Hitler's speeches. But Hitler was hiding something from his friend: the Vienna Academy of Fine Arts had rejected his test drawings and turned down his application. He'd been so sure of his future as an artist that the rejection hit him "like a bolt from the blue," he later wrote. Shaken and ashamed, Hitler had even kept it a secret from his mother, and stayed on in Vienna, pretending to go to school.

The play-acting couldn't last forever. Hitler received a second blow when his mother died, months after he had failed the entrance exam. Drifting without a goal, Hitler soon fell out of touch with his sister and with Kubizek. When his money ran out, he moved from his cheap room into a hostel for homeless men.

For a couple of years Hitler lived off the pennies he made selling his watercolor postcards of street scenes. His life was a far cry from his image of himself as a great artist. In his bitterness he did not have to look far for someone to blame. Vienna had long been the center of Austria's once-powerful empire, but it was going through radical changes. Its population had swelled, and now fewer than half of its residents had been born in the capital. Many of the newcomers were Czechs, Poles, and Jews. Among Vienna's German population were some who felt threatened by change and by the newcomers. The city was full of pamphlets and newspapers that blamed Jews for society's problems, and Hitler had nothing but time on his hands in which to brood over them.

Still aimless, Hitler slipped out of Austria into the German province of Bavaria to avoid being drafted into the army when he turned 21. In the Bavarian capital, Munich, he peddled his paintings and read at night. He felt withdrawn from others and angry at the world.

The outbreak of World War I in 1914 changed Hitler's life. Like thousands of others in Munich, Hitler greeted the war with excitement and a sense of German patriotism. The bitter reality of war would soon change their minds, but for now the air was charged with enthusiasm. Hitler volunteered for the Bavarian army.

In a corner of his regiment's command post, three kilometers (two miles) from the front, Corporal Hitler sat with his head sunk in a newspaper, ignoring the jokes of his fellow soldiers. Although they liked Hitler well enough, they found him odd, with his brooding eyes and pale, sunken cheeks. He never got packages or letters, and stayed tight-lipped when the others chatted about their girlfriends or families. The only creature he showed affection to was a stray dog that had wandered across the lines. Hitler rarely smiled, but his comrades knew they could always get a rise out of him by mentioning defeat. That would send him into a rage. "For us the war cannot be lost!" he would insist.

For Hitler, life in a regiment provided everything he had been searching for—not only regular meals and daily discipline, but also a cause. He enjoyed being among soldiers, where he could be a loner but not completely alone. And he experienced some success in the army.

Within months of enlisting, Hitler was promoted to corporal and made a dispatch runner, taking messages from staff headquarters to the front. He was even awarded the Iron Cross for bravery. However, he was never promoted again—his commanding officers felt he lacked leadership qualities.

Being a dispatch runner may have kept Hitler out of the trenches, but it did not protect him completely. He was crouching in a dugout with other runners when the hole was flooded with mustard gas. Hitler was temporarily blinded. He was sent back to German territory to recover. Lying in his hospital bed, he heard shocking news: Germany had lost the war, and a revolution had toppled its monarchy from power. The kaiser was gone; the country was now a republic.

Hitler's first reaction to the news of defeat was despair, then anger. He also knew he had nothing to go home to now that the war was over. Luckily for Hitler, he was able to remain in what was left of the army. Back in Munich, he was trained as a propaganda agent. The army felt that too many returning soldiers sounded sympathetic to the ideas of Russian Communists. Hitler and his fellow instructors were sent to an army camp to teach the troops more nationalistic ideas and to stay on the lookout for troublemakers.

Hitler threw himself into his new work, and it was now that he discovered his true talent: public speaking. In the barracks lecture rooms, audiences of bored soldiers were roused by the raw emotion in his words, the gritty language he used—and by his absolute conviction that he was right.

The army sent Hitler, now 30, to a meeting of the German Workers' Party. This new party preached the kind of nationalism the army liked; maybe putting one of their own agents on the inside would help it grow. At the meeting, Hitler got into a debate with one of the speakers. The party's leaders were awed by the heated way Hitler attacked his opponent. "Goodness, he's got a mouth. We could use him," the party chairman exclaimed. They invited Hitler to join.

I must have a crowd when I speak. In a small, intimate circle I never know what to say.
—Hitler

Hitler saw an opportunity: one person could make a difference in such a small group, maybe even control it. He was soon speaking for the party, and instead of holding tiny meetings in dingy pubs, the group was packing beer halls with crowds drawn by Hitler's explosive, angry speeches. Standing on one of the long wooden tables, dressed in a shabby suit, Hitler hammered upon his themes: Germany, once strong, was now weak and divided. The peace treaty it had signed at the end of the war was an insult, designed to leave the country helpless and bankrupt. The country was being taken over by Communists. Common workers were exploited by Jewish profiteers.

The Munich audience had heard all this before; they were the complaints of many fringe political parties. But Hitler's presentation was much more exciting.

Hitler played on his audience's fears, catering to their hopes with vague promises and reducing complicated problems to simple terms of black and white. As his attacks got harsher, he began to shout—and was interrupted frequently by applause and cheers. By the end of the speech—which might last two hours—the audience was wild. At last Hitler had found something to replace his broken dream of becoming an artist: politics.

And who was listening? Inside the packed halls were students, soldiers, workers, and office people. Most were young and liked Hitler's radical talk. Many of them felt humiliated by Germany's defeat and frightened for the country's future, as well as their own. A handful of Hitler's listeners had connections that he did not. Wealthy supporters provided access to social circles closed to Hitler, where the party could raise money. A junior officer named Ernst Röhm became Hitler's link to sympathetic officers in the military.

Hitler urged the German Workers' Party to be controversial. The well-publicized meetings were packed with both followers and opponents, and shouting matches kept the atmosphere electric. In 1920 he chose an attention-grabbing banner for the party: a hooked black cross known as a swastika in a white circle on a red background.

By 1922, Hitler was drawing as many as 50,000 to rallies for the party, now known as the National Socialist German Workers' Party. Hermann Göring, a famous World War I combat pilot, also joined. Vain and ambitious, Göring gave the movement new prestige. With Göring and the dependable Röhm, Hitler began to recruit private troops, the *Sturmabteilung* (Storm Detachment), or SA for short. Their job was to control the crowds at rallies and bully political opponents.

STABBED IN THE BACK?

Hitler was an opportunist who could exploit a crisis to bring people over to his side. He made the most of the problems rocking Germany in the 1920s and 1930s to get into power. Skyrocketing inflation in the 1920s meant that it took 6 billion marks to equal one pre-war mark. A sausage roll might cost 4 billion marks! It became hard to feed a family even on a "good" salary. Then, in the 1930s, the Depression left millions unemployed. Through it all, many people distrusted Germany's new democracy, which seemed power-less to solve the country's prob-lems. The monarchy was not far in the past, and some longed for one ruler to take control again. Hitler offered himself as that leader.

One of his most powerful messages was a promise to smash the hated Versailles treaty. While people had called the First World War "the war to end all wars," critics of the peace treaty signed at its end called that docu-ment "the peace to end all peace." In signing the Treaty of Versailles in 1919, Germany took responsibility for the war. It was forced t make huge payments in cash and resources to the victors, reduce its armed forces, give up territories, and accept occupation forces in some regions. The terms were so harsh that some feared they would provoke a backlash.

Many German soldiers re-called that they did not feel they were on the verge of defeat when the war ended. This helped fuel the idea that the brave troops at the front had been "stabbed in the back" by politicians in the new democracy at home, which had surrendered. They had been urged to do so, the story went, by the Jews, who had stayed away from the front and made money from the war. It was all a myth (in fact many Jews had fought bravely for Germany), but a convincing one for many—the Jews had long been convenient scapegoats for grumblers. Hitler took full advan-tage of these false beliefs. "The art of all great popular leaders," he said, "consisted at all times in concentrating the attention of the masses on a single enemy."

Hitler's pet ideas—confirmed by his scattered reading in history and politics—had now hardened into a set of beliefs that would change little over the years: Life was a struggle; the strong overcame the weak. Germany's future depended on gaining more territory, to be achieved by expanding eastward. A life-and-death battle with Communism was coming. Communism's twin evil was the Jewish people. In Hitler's view, Jews were not real Germans at all. To be great again, Germans must keep their race "pure."

By 1923, the time seemed ripe for action. Nazi party membership had swelled; that year 35,000 new people joined. The 3,000 storm troopers under Göring were straining like dogs on a leash. Hitler and the party decided on a bold gamble. They would take over the Bavarian government in a *putsch*—a violent uprising—then march to Berlin.

Hitler saw his chance when Bavaria's government leaders organized a rally in one of Munich's largest beer halls. While Hitler waited quietly inside and crowds filled the hall, truckloads of Nazi storm troopers arrived to surround the building. On cue, Hitler climbed onto a chair and fired his pistol at the ceiling. "The national revolution has broken out!" he shouted. "The hall is surrounded!"

The plan was to escort the government leaders to another room and persuade them to join the cause, but things did not go smoothly. Someone managed to call for the army to put down the rebels. The Beer Hall Putsch, as it became known, ended with Hitler being arrested for treason. But he found he had sympathizers among the police and the judges at his trial, where he scored a publicity triumph.

The courtroom was his chance to speak to a national audience: newspapers from all over Germany were following the trial. His loyal troops were merging into battalions, Hitler declared. They would smash Germany's enemies and make it great again. "You might just as well find us guilty a thousand times," he told the judges, "but the goddess of the eternal court of history will smile and tear up … the judgment of this court: for she finds us not guilty."

Hitler's light sentence—five years at a low-security prison—was a strong hint that the judges at least partly shared his views. In the end, he served less than a year. And he had learned a valuable lesson from his trial. He was attracting attention and support. Maybe a violent takeover wasn't necessary. Maybe power could be his legally—through the ballot box.

By the time Hitler was released from prison, Germany's economy was booming and the future looked good. As a result, interest in the radical Nazis was at a low point. Hitler, banned for a time from public speaking, was back on the margins of society. But in 1929 the U.S. stock market crash triggered a worldwide disaster: the Great Depression. By the early 1930s, over 5 million Germans were unemployed—and desperate. It was the crisis Hitler needed to rekindle interest in his party.

Crisis was Hitler's oxygen. He needed it to survive.
—Ian Kershaw, historian and Hitler biographer

Arguments within the Nazi party as to who should lead it ended with the charismatic Hitler the clear winner. During the 1932 elections, the Nazis went all out in an effort to put him at the front of every voter's mind. The streets were filled with marching SA troops under red-and-black flags; meetings and rallies were scheduled non-stop. Hitler chartered a plane and flew from city to city. Posters proclaimed, *Our Last Hope: Hitler.*

The massive propaganda effort paid off: the Nazis became the largest party in the Reichstag, Germany's parliament. A few months later, powerful business leaders convinced President Hindenburg to appoint Hitler Reich chancellor, the second most important position in the government. Better Hitler than Communists who would force unions on them, the business leaders reasoned. They expected that the radical Hitler would be tamed in government. They couldn't have been more wrong.

THE BIG LIE:
THE ART OF PROPAGANDA

Propaganda—the attempt to manipulate the opinions of a population—was an art Hitler pursued with a vengeance. It was central to his success in getting votes and staying in power. Once he controlled every form of communication and source of information—from newspapers and radio to local clubs and school texts—Hitler could spread his message like no leader before him. His propaganda minister, Joseph Goebbels, labored to build a cult around Hitler himself, one that worshiped him as Germany's savior. The Nazis also worked to create the illusion that the vast majority agreed with everything they did. This meant silencing opposition (no one could criticize Hitler in speeches or in print) and filling the press, radio, and cinemas with approving comments on the regime.

Nazi propaganda was at its most dramatic in mass rallies. Swept up in the enthusiasm of the crowd and

Hitler shone at seizing opportunities, and within a month of his becoming chancellor his moment arrived. On a February night in 1933, a young Communist set fire to the Reichstag building as a protest against capitalism. Hitler jumped on the excuse to declare a state of emergency. Göring ordered mass arrests of Communists. Personal rights were suspended, including freedom of speech, freedom of the press, and freedom of association. Political prisoners could be held in "protective custody" for an unlimited time without trial. A month later the first concentration camp was opened near Dachau. Its first inmates would be the outlawed Communists.

impressed by the show of strength, a single person was, in Goebbels's words, turned "from a little worm into part of a large dragon." People felt as if they were participating in something huge and important, which helped them forget that they had lost any say in their government.

Propaganda was also used to make evil easier for people to accept. The Nazis repeatedly described their supposed enemies—Jews, Communists, Slavs—not as people but as "rats," "parasites," and "diseases." Once people stopped thinking of these groups as human beings, it was easier to be ruthless.

> *The broad masses of a nation ... more readily fall victim to a big lie than to a small one.*
> —Hitler

Hitler believed in a few key rules for powerful propaganda: Keep it simple. Repeat points over and over. Always appeal to groups and the "herd instinct," not to individuals. Don't try to persuade with rational arguments. Appeal to the most basic emotions, especially fear and hate.

While Hitler's political opponents had been crushed, another potential threat was emerging within the Nazi party itself. The SA, whose brute force had been useful on the climb to power, were now a problem. Germany's army leaders were not happy about being second in line to the storm troopers. Hitler knew he needed the army's support; if their loyalty went elsewhere, he could be toppled from power. The SA for their part resented the growing powers of a rival Nazi police force, the *Schutzstaffel* (Protection Squad), or SS. Starting as Hitler's personal bodyguards, the SS had grown into an elite force, now led by an efficient and ruthless Nazi party member, Heinrich Himmler.

Göring and Himmler were keen to nip the arrogant SA. Hitler worried that betraying his right-hand man Röhm would tarnish his image. But he finally agreed. On the night of June 30, 1934, the SS arrested 85 or more SA leaders, including Röhm, accused them of planning a coup, and shot them on the spot. In what became known as the Night of the Long Knives, Hitler showed the world how ruthless he could be, even to his own supporters.

Within a few weeks, Hitler was able to gather even more power into his hands. In August the elderly Hindenburg died. The offices of president and chancellor were merged, and all soldiers swore an oath of loyalty to Hitler personally. Army leaders hoped this would bind the armed forces closer to the new head of state, increasing their own authority.

With a speed that was breathtaking, Hitler had crushed opposition, suspended civil rights, surrounded himself with a powerful personal guard, become supreme commander of the armed forces, and made himself undisputed *Führer*—"Leader"—of Germany.

On May 10, 1933, Nazi storm troopers and German university students staged book burnings around the country. Any writings that contradicted Nazi ideas were thrown into the bonfires—including novels, histories, poetry, and works of philosophy. The largest burning took place in Berlin (above), where 20,000 books went up in flames.

Once in power, Hitler fell into the idle habits of his youth. He divided his time between his residence in Berlin and a country retreat he had bought in the Bavarian Alps. But at neither place did he keep a disciplined routine. He worked on and off, sleeping late and rarely speaking to his staff before lunch. This was often a bland meal, since Hitler, a vegetarian who didn't drink alcohol, liked to keep his food simple. Evenings were devoted to films or music, especially Wagner. After that, Hitler might labor until the early hours on a speech.

I always go to the very brink of boldness, but not beyond. One has to smell out: What can I get away with, and what can't I?
—Hitler

Cabinet meetings became rare, and finally Hitler stopped meeting officially with his ministers altogether. Soon his casual remarks at lunch or dinner were being noted and taken away to be translated into orders. Hitler was happy to let his ministers fight among themselves about how the Führer's will should be put into action. Competition would keep them striving to please and prevent them from forming alliances against him.

Hitler, for so long a loner, now found himself surrounded by supporters. Yet few of them felt they were close to him. He began spending time with his photographer's assistant, Eva Braun, a girl 23 years younger than himself. She was loyal and undemanding, as Hitler believed a woman should be. But he refused to be seen with her in public. His image as a bachelor, Hitler claimed, had been important in getting women's votes. Others suspected that Hitler simply had trouble having a close relationship with anyone.

His leadership may have seemed disorganized, but Hitler was taking decisive steps towards his goals. In 1935 he began building up the German army with forced military service. The following year he ordered that the army and economy be ready for war in four years.

In 1936, Hitler took a huge gamble. Ignoring Göring's concerns, he decided to send troops into the Rhineland. The Versailles treaty had declared this strip of land on Germany's western border off limits to the German military. Hitler suffered from stomach cramps and sleepless nights beforehand. What would France and its ally Great Britain do if he broke the treaty? But the gamble paid off. The other countries took no action. Fear of starting another war made them stop short of using force. In Germany, Hitler was more popular than ever.

Success made Hitler bold. He turned next to one of his dearest goals: *Lebensraum*—"living space" for the German people. He had long preached that ethnic Germans, now scattered throughout Europe, deserved to be part of one strong German Reich. And that Reich, Hitler believed, could only be great if it controlled enough space. "Germany will either be a world power," Hitler wrote, "or there will be no Germany."

In March 1938, German troops crossed the border into Hitler's homeland of Austria, which was declared part of the German Reich. Hitler's motorcade paraded triumphantly through Vienna, the Führer standing in his open-top car. A jubilant pro-German crowd cheered his arrival. He savored the moment. The last time he had stood in this place, he recalled with satisfaction, he had been a penniless artist.

Much of Europe was alarmed by these "bloodless victories," as they were called. It looked as if Czechoslovakia could be next. Three million Germans lived in a part of Czechoslovakia known as the Sudetenland, and Hitler demanded to rescue this "persecuted minority."

European leaders met in Munich to decide Czechoslovakia's fate. No one wanted to plunge Europe into another war. It was agreed that Germany could occupy the Sudetenland. "It is the last territorial demand I will make in Europe," Hitler assured the other leaders. Hitler also agreed to sign a declaration that Britain and Germany intended never to go to war with each other again. Back in England, Prime Minister Neville Chamberlain waved the document as he stepped off the airplane from Germany. He had achieved, he said, "peace in our time."

Within a month, Hitler issued a secret order to prepare for the conquest of the rest of Czechoslovakia.

CAPTURING YOUNG MINDS

A Nazi poster urges young Germans: "Youth serves the Führer: All 10-year-olds into the Hitler Youth."

While the expansion of Hitler's Reich across Europe was underway, he and his henchmen tightened their grip on potential opponents inside Germany.

On November 9 and 10, 1938, a wave of violence erupted across the country, as hundreds of Jewish shops were looted and synagogues set on fire. So many store windows were shattered that the rampage became

A central Nazi goal was to shape the beliefs of young people early, especially through clubs such as the Hitler Youth. Among the ideas drummed into members was complete obedience to the Führer and the glory of dying for him. Membership for boys and girls aged 10 to 18 became mandatory, and by 1939 nearly 9 million young people belonged. After-school club activities prepared boys for the military and girls for motherhood. Boys spent time marching, pistol shooting, crawling under barbed wire, and throwing grenades. Girls marched, ran, swam, and learned to make a bed.

Schooling was also transformed to complete the Nazi training. In history class, students were told that Jewish and Communist spies had caused Germany's defeat in World War I. In biology they studied the sham Nazi science of race, which justified Hitler's claim that Germans were superior. Students learned about the supposed differences between races and how to choose a good mate in order to have racially pure children. Physical education was stressed. Boxing became compulsory for boys, and failing a fitness test could get a student expelled.

Hitler wanted to mold young Germans to be "as swift as greyhounds, as tough as leather, and as hard as steel." The goal was to create a new generation of obedient Germans convinced of Nazi ideals.

known as *Kristallnacht,* The Night of Broken Glass. The excuse for the incident was the murder of a German official at the Paris embassy by a Jewish college student. Hitler—always careful about his public image—did not order the anti-Jewish backlash, but he let his propaganda minister, Joseph Goebbels, know that he would not disapprove of any public demonstrations. Goebbels took the hint. The destruction was supposed to look like an unplanned series of protests, but it had been engineered by Goebbels himself.

Following Kristallnacht, new restrictions were imposed designed to drive the Jews out of Germany's economy by barring them from professions and keeping them from doing business. They went even further than the Nuremberg Laws of 1935, which had already turned Jews into social outsiders, forbidding them to marry non-Jews and depriving them of many rights.

The German Jews were not the only ones who did

THE FINAL SOLUTION

From his earliest campaigns Hitler had said that he wanted the Jews out of Europe, but he did not specify how this would happen. Beginning with laws and persecutions designed to drive German Jews out of the country, Hitler's "war against the Jews" escalated.

Early on, Hitler talked of deporting the whole Jewish population to somewhere outside the Reich. During World War II, Jews in conquered countries such as Poland were herded into ghettos. Special squads followed the German army as it marched eastward into Russia, rounding up Jews to be executed. Finally, concentration camps were set up, connected by railways, where inmates either died from forced labor or were killed in poison-gas chambers.

Hitler was concerned with his public image and with how he would be viewed by history. And so throughout the war he avoided writing direct orders for the killing of Jews—a program that became known as the Holocaust. Instead, he gave vague verbal instructions to willing henchmen such as Heinrich Himmler and Reinhard Heydrich of the SS.

not fit into Hitler's vision for a "pure" Germany. Gypsies, homosexuals, and opponents of all kinds were persecuted. The Nazis also put in motion a secret program of euthanasia—"mercy killings"— to rid the country of what they called "useless eaters": people with mental and physical handicaps, those with hereditary diseases, anyone unable to work. In the regime's chilling new language, the German people as a whole were a body, one that had to be kept healthy; Jews and "misfits" were diseases that must be destroyed to save the patient.

As victory moved beyond Hitler's grasp, the war against the Jews was stepped up, as something that could be won. By 1945 the Nazis' "final solution to the Jewish question" had resulted in the killing of 6 million European Jews.

Polish Jews are rounded up by German soldiers in the Warsaw Ghetto, 1943.

In the hour before dawn on a September morning in 1939, the sky along the German-Polish border lit up with artillery fire. German troops and tanks surged onto Polish territory shortly afterwards. Overhead, waves of dive-bombers and fighter planes filled the skies. A new kind of warfare was being unleashed. *Blitzkrieg*—"lightning war"—was designed to overwhelm with speed and violence. Germany did not declare war on Poland until the attack was well underway.

The rest of Europe had watched Hitler grow more aggressive. He always justified his ambitions: Germany was acting in self-defense; his hand was being forced. His most recent complaints had been about the Polish Corridor, a strip of land belonging to Poland that separated East Prussia from the rest of Germany. Alarmed, Poland had asked Britain and France to guarantee they would come to its aid in the case of an invasion. But Hitler gambled that Britain would not go to war over Poland, as it had not for Czechoslovakia. "Our enemies are small worms. I saw them in Munich," Hitler remarked to his generals.

Hitler's SS had staged phony attacks on German buildings near the border, claiming they had been carried out by Poles. Hitler then summoned his generals to his country retreat in the Alps. Instructing them not to take notes, he spoke openly about his intention to attack. "The victor will not be asked afterwards whether he told the truth or not," he lectured them. "When starting and waging a war, it is not right that matters, but victory. Close your hearts to pity. Act brutally. Eighty million people must obtain what is their right." The generals were grim. One thought Hitler sounded like someone "determined to leap into the dark." But no one objected.

To keep the Soviet Union from interfering with his

plans for Poland, Hitler had signed a pact with the Communist leader, Joseph Stalin, promising they would not wage war against each other. They secretly agreed to divide Poland and the Baltic nations between them. But Hitler never intended to honor the treaty. Russia's vast lands were, in his mind, the ultimate expanse of living space his empire needed.

Hitler also told his generals that the war against Poland—and later Russia—would be a different kind of war. This was the land of Slavs, people he had long preached were inferior to Germans. He ordered his commanders to "Germanize" the territory. This was "a war of extermination."

The streets of Paris were empty in the early morning hours, their silence broken only by the hum of three speeding Mercedes sedans. Sitting in the first car next to his driver was Hitler, touring the capital he had conquered. He had brought along his architect, Albert Speer. They began at five-thirty and would finish before nine—a whirlwind tour of a city of monuments.

It was June 1940, and Hitler's armies had triumphed over France in four weeks. He was at the height of his power. With the quick fall of Poland followed by that of France, the doubts of his generals were put to rest. "My Führer," one fawned, "you are the greatest military commander of all time!" When the French government asked for a truce, Hitler slapped his thigh for joy: it was time for revenge. The train car in which the German generals of World War I had surrendered was dragged out of its museum and placed where it had stood in 1918. There, Hitler watched in silent satisfaction as the French surrendered.

Seeing Paris had once been the dream of his life, the untraveled Hitler told Speer. "In the past I often considered whether we would not have to destroy Paris," he said. "But when we are finished in Berlin, Paris will be only a shadow. So why would we destroy it?" On their return to Germany, Hitler gave Speer the task of rebuilding Berlin on a scale never seen before. It was to be the capital of a Reich that would last a thousand years, Hitler declared, the crowning glory of his vision for the post-war world. In that world, an educated German elite would lead an advanced society that stretched from western Europe to the farthest reaches of Russia. German soldier-farmers would colonize the vast conquered territories. Defeated nations would furnish oil, grain, and steel while their inferior races provided slave labor. Already, gangs of forced laborers from defeated countries had been shipped to work in Germany, building roads, tanks, and airplanes for the victors.

The conquered peoples should be kept poor and uneducated, Hitler believed. "Let them know just enough to understand our highway signs," he advised, "so that they won't get themselves run over by our vehicles."

In late winter 1943, Hitler prepared to meet with his military commanders at his gloomy headquarters in the woods of East Prussia, a complex nicknamed the Wolf's Lair. Their conversations were tense now, and Hitler looked exhausted. Göring noticed that Hitler seemed to have aged 15 years since the start of the war.

Hitler's string of victories was over. His blitzkrieg had failed to conquer Russia. Britain had not given up and negotiated for peace, as Hitler had hoped, and the

HITLER'S CONQUESTS: EUROPE 1942

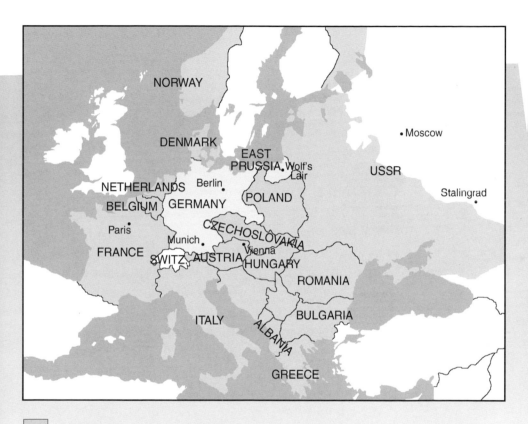

◻ areas controlled by Nazi Germany and its allies (including Italy, Hungary, Romania, and Bulgaria)

◻ original German territory

By 1942, the Nazi occupation of Europe had reached its height. Hitler's armies had pushed to their farthest point inside Russia, while Germany and its allies dominated most of the continent, from Norway to North Africa.

United States had entered the war against him. Events had slipped out of his control. Now, Hitler was gambling more wildly, insisting that "will power" could bring victory where strategy had not. Looking for scapegoats to blame for his defeats, he stripped military leaders of their ranks and took personal command of the army. A gulf opened between Hitler and his generals.

The subject of the winter meeting was the recent defeat of Germany's army at Stalingrad, in the Soviet Union. The battle for the city had turned into a nightmare. Savage fighting at close range for streets and buildings had killed huge numbers on both sides. The Soviet army had surrounded what was left of the German army in Stalingrad. Cut off from help, the German troops were freezing, starving, and under heavy fire. But Hitler refused their general's request to retreat or to attempt a breakout. Hitler ordered them to stand their ground, "to the last soldier and the last bullet." With his stubborn order Hitler guaranteed the death or capture of nearly 220,000 men.

At the meeting with his generals, Hitler said nothing about the loss of so many German lives in Stalingrad. Instead he raged about the surrender of their general to the Russians. He should have shot himself, Hitler declared, like the commanders of old who fell on their swords when all was lost.

The war had turned sour, but the Nazis kept Germany flooded with propaganda, coloring all newsreels with heroic scenes from the front. Germans had been told victory at Stalingrad was just around the corner. When news of the defeat was revealed, newsstands were swarmed by screaming crowds. And for the first time during the war, criticisms were aimed at Hitler himself.

"Hitler cannot win the war; he can only prolong it," proclaimed a pamphlet written by a lone resistance group of German students. It was a brave but futile act, and the students were beheaded for treason. But some in the military agreed. In 1944 a group of German officers concluded that Germany was headed for destruction. Its only hope was to kill Hitler and negotiate peace. Time was short. The alliance of countries fighting Hitler—including the United States, England, and Canada—had successfully landed forces on the beaches of Normandy. The Allied advance into France had begun.

Security was tight around Hitler, who spent almost all his time at the Wolf's Lair. But the plotters' chance arrived when one of them was promoted to a rank that let him into Hitler's closed military meetings. Colonel Claus von Stauffenberg arrived at Hitler's daily military conference with a bomb in his briefcase. Its delay mechanism would give him 15 minutes to get away before it went off. He slipped in next to Hitler, who was studying a map on a table. Stauffenberg set the briefcase down and nudged it under the table with his foot. Then he waited as long as he could before muttering an excuse and stepping outside.

Minutes later, an explosion tore through the headquarters. Stauffenberg saw the smoke and flying debris. The colonel flew to Berlin, where a military takeover by the other conspirators was supposed to be already underway. He was horrified to discover it had not gone ahead. Hitler was still alive. After Stauffenberg left, someone had bumped into his briefcase, knocking it away from the Führer. The explosion ruptured Hitler's eardrum and left him with a shaking right arm, but it did not kill him.

That night, Hitler spoke to the nation on the radio. His voice unusually quiet, he promised that the "tiny clique" of conspirators would be rooted out. The assassination attempt confirmed in Hitler's mind a suspicion he had long held: he could not trust his generals. "Now I know why all my great plans in Russia had to fail in recent years. It was all treason!" he raged before his aides. "But for those traitors, we would have won long ago." In a sweeping crackdown, suspected plotters and opponents of the regime—5,000 in all—were arrested. Two hundred were executed, including eight high-ranking officers.

Hitler gave the go-ahead to mobilize the country for total war. Arms production went into high gear, and with the forced labor of prisoners of war and conquered civilians, tanks and guns were produced faster than ever. All males from 16 to 60 were drafted into the "people's army." But the Allies were now bombing Germany's cities around the clock, and their armies were closing in. The Nazis could only push people to fight and hold out.

Hitler cut himself off from the world. He had always kept other people's suffering at arm's length, never visiting a concentration camp or army hospital. But he had become more isolated recently. With no victories to proclaim, he avoided the public, and he stayed clear of the German cities devastated by Allied bombs.

Then, in a sudden burst of energy, Hitler roused himself for one last effort to turn the war around. His plan was daring and had the element of surprise, he told his commanders, and it would snatch the initiative back from Allied hands. By mustering every man and tank they could, the Germans would attempt to drive a wedge between the American and British troops in

Belgium, near the German border. They would wait for bad weather, when Allied planes would be unable to protect the troops on the ground.

Hitler's bold gambles had succeeded before, but this was an act of desperation. Despite early success, the attack—known as the Battle of the Bulge—was doomed once the weather cleared and Allied planes were able to fire on the German forces. Defeat for Germany, and for Hitler, was now only a matter of time.

HITLER: FACTS

Born: April 20, 1889
Died: April 30, 1945
Name at birth: Adolf Hitler
Titles in power: Reich Chancellor, 1933–34; Führer, 1934–45
Age upon coming to power: 43
Time in power: 12 years
Size of domain: In 1942, Germany and its allies occupied Europe from Norway to the Mediterranean Sea, and from France to the outskirts of Stalingrad in the Soviet Union.
Armed forces commanded: German army, the *Wehrmacht*, around 10 million men by 1944
Number of victims: Historians estimate 18 million.
Defining characteristics: egotistical, hateful, convinced of his own greatness and mission, charismatic
Legacy: Plunged the world into a war that claimed as many as 40 million lives. Conducted a genocide that destroyed 64 percent of Europe's Jews. Left Germany defeated and divided in two, the eastern half dominated by the Soviet Union until 1990.

Deep in a bunker under the garden at his Berlin head-
quarters, Hitler crouched down to inspect at eye level
an architectural model. It was a proposal for the new
city center of Linz, his hometown. Hitler remained
focused on it, ignoring the messengers who stood waiting with bad news from the front. Reality was becoming
hard to face.

Bombing had forced Hitler and his staff down into
the bunker, an air-raid shelter that had been expanded
into an underground complex. No daylight
reached them there, and fresh air had to be
pumped in with fans. Day and night blurred
together. Pale in the artificial light, the
bunker's residents were cut off from the
world above and far from the war. In late
night talks, Hitler rambled on for hours as
his staff tried to keep their eyes open. He outlined his
grand plans for post-war Germany or fondly recalled
the party's old days of struggle. His limbs shook, and he
was unable to sleep.

We'll not capitulate. Never! We may go down, but we'll take a world with us.
—Hitler

Of his old allies, only Goebbels remained with him.
Above-ground, Göring and Himmler were scrambling
to secure a future for themselves after the regime. In
Hitler's absence, Göring had tried to name himself the
Führer's successor. Himmler hoped to negotiate peace
terms with the Allies. Hitler denounced both as traitors.

From the map room of the bunker, Hitler directed
the final defense of Berlin. Those with him were nervous;
within moments Hitler's mood could swing from joy to
rage to deep depression. He clung to the far-fetched
idea that some twist of fate might turn the war around.
Perhaps the Soviet army's advance across eastern
Europe would scare the other Allies. Britain and France
might want to join with Germany to fight Communism

together. At other times he placed his hopes in the "wonder weapons" his armaments ministry had built, such as a rocket-driven bomb he could launch against Britain. Although a handful of rockets were fired, they had little impact on the war.

The one option he refused to consider was negotiation of peace terms. Better to die fighting, and all of Germany with him, than to give in. He blamed the German people for deserving their destruction. Hadn't they proved the weaker race in the struggle for survival? "If the German people loses the war, it will have proved itself not worthy of me," he said. Hitler seemed determined to play the part of one of Wagner's heroes in the operas he loved, betrayed and destined to go up in flames that would burn the world as well. In a rage, he ordered the destruction of all transportation, communications, industry, arms—in short, "all resources within the Reich." Only ruins should await the invading enemy. But his power to enforce this order aboveground was gone.

Hitler surfaced one last time to pin Iron Cross medals on a group of boys who were defending Berlin against Soviet tanks. Reports arrived that Berlin could not hold out for more than 24 hours, then that Russian troops were a street away. Hitler dictated his will. Was there any sign of remorse for the suffering he had caused, any regrets expressed in his last words? It would seem not. History would prove him right, he insisted.

He had no intention of allowing the Soviets to parade him around as a humiliated captive. Not even his body should be left for them to use. He planned to commit suicide, and then his aides were to burn his remains beyond recognition. Hitler retreated to a private room with Eva Braun. Impressed by her loyalty, he had married her in the bunker two days before. Now he shot himself with his pistol while his wife swallowed poison. Seven days later, a devastated Germany surrendered to the Allied armies.

Hitler's "thousand-year Reich" had lasted only 12 years. "As long as the German nation yields to one individual will," he had once promised, "all problems will be solved." And millions were prepared to believe him.

STALIN
REVOLUTION FROM ABOVE

Iran, 1943

The Soviet Union had been battling German invaders for two terrible years, in what Russians would call the Great Patriotic War and Western countries would know as World War II. Russia and its allies, Great Britain and the United States, could at last see victory against Hitler within reach. It would take two more years to get there.

The Soviet leader, Joseph Stalin, was about to meet face to face with British prime minister Winston Churchill and U.S. president Franklin Roosevelt. Stalin desperately needed them to challenge the Germans on a second European front, drawing part of Hitler's armies out of Russia to weaken the onslaught. However, he did not trust his allies. For a long time he would not agree to any of the suggested locations for the meeting; he stubbornly refused anywhere far from Russia. Only near his military staff, close to the seat of his power in Moscow, did he feel secure. Finally he agreed to Tehran, not far from Russia's southern border.

I trust no one, not even myself.
—Joseph Stalin

Stalin traveled to the meeting by plane, and flying so terrified him that he vowed never to do it again. Just before takeoff he switched planes with his subordinates, nervously choosing the aircraft flown by the higher-ranking pilot. The escort of 27 fighter planes did little to reassure him, and he grew frantic when the plane hit turbulence.

At the meeting, the leaders were aware that their alliance was unnatural, forced upon them by circumstances. Churchill and Roosevelt were wary of becoming allies of a dictator such as Stalin; but as Churchill said, they would "make a deal with the devil" to defeat a worse evil —Adolf Hitler. Stalin could not have been more different from the other two leaders. Churchill, born in Blenheim Palace, was tied to the old aristocracy of England. Roosevelt came from the newer world of American landowners and industrialists. Across the conference table from them, rigid in his marshal's uniform, sat Stalin: the son of peasants, born in a one-room shack in a remote province of Russia. He saw the other two first and foremost as capitalists, the enemies of a Communist like himself. Around them, Stalin was stiff and unsmiling. He relaxed only when he glimpsed disagreement between his two allies. Churchill, Stalin later said, would pick your pocket for a *kopek* (penny), while Roosevelt would dip his hand in only for bigger coins.

Uneasy allies: Joseph Stalin (left) with U.S. president Roosevelt and British prime minister Churchill outside the Russian embassy in Tehran. They were brought together by a common goal—to defeat Adolf Hitler.

Once the conference was over, Stalin was relieved to return to his native soil. He quickly changed from his military uniform into his old overcoat and boots, and sped in an armored train to Moscow. Meanwhile, the British and American governments were busy convincing their people at home that Stalin was a friend and ally. American newspapers nicknamed him "Uncle Joe," a lovable Russian with his bushy mustache and pipe. Yet the same Uncle Joe had by this time executed and imprisoned millions of his own people.

Joseph Stalin began life as Joseph Dzhugashvili. The world he was born into in the winter of 1879 had changed little in centuries. His small town lay in Georgia, a poor and isolated area southwest of Russia, near Turkey and the Black Sea. The country had been taken over by Russia, an empire ruled by a czar and a wealthy upper class. Most of the empire's population— 80 percent—were uneducated peasants who farmed the land.

Joseph's own parents were freed serfs, once tied by law to the land they worked and to its owner. Joseph, strong and wiry, was the first of their children to survive. Soso, as he was nicknamed, proved tough enough to endure a harsh childhood—including a bout of small-pox that scarred his face for life, and an accident that crushed his left arm, leaving it weaker than the right.

His father, a cobbler who could not make a living from his trade, was often drunk and violent. Stalin's deeply religious mother was unable to protect her son from his father's rages. From a young age Soso learned to be wary and distrustful, always on the lookout for signs of anger from his father. With a craftiness beyond his years, he hid his feelings to stay out of trouble. But Joseph had a rebellious streak, too, once striking back during his father's attack by throwing a knife.

Soso's mother could not read, and she made ends meet by doing people's washing. She had one dream: that her smart son would one day become a priest. She scrounged for money to send him to the seminary in Tiflis, Georgia's capital. It was the closest thing to a university the city had. There, boys were trained to become priests in the Russian Orthodox Church.

Once at the seminary, however, teenage Joseph took a different path. His rebellious side was deepened by life at the school, an atmosphere that was part monastery, part barracks. The teachers spied on the students and searched their clothes, forever reporting suspicious activity to the principal. His schoolmates could see how cynical Joseph's troubled home life had made him. He tended to look on the bad side, one friend recalled, and had no faith in people's good intentions.

During their short breaks from studying, Joseph and some other students sometimes smuggled forbidden books from the public library back to their rooms. Reading under his bedcovers at night, Joseph discovered the ideas of Karl Marx. This German writer predicted that workers would someday rise up and replace the business and factory owners who took advantage of them. A new world order, with the workers in charge, would be brought about by a violent revolution. Marx also rejected religion, calling it a tool to keep oppressed workers in line. Joseph was instantly won over by these ideas, which he took very personally. "Since all people in authority over others seemed to him to be like his father," one of his schoolmates later said, "there soon arose in him a vengeful feeling against all people standing above him."

Joseph began to look around him at the city outside the seminary. In past years huge numbers of workers had been pouring into Tiflis for jobs at the area's new railroads, mines, and factories. Their living conditions were often overcrowded and dirty, their work dangerous and underpaid. Many of them had radical political ideas about changing things. Some had started illegal revolutionary groups that met in secret. Joseph soon joined a group of young Marxists.

Reading forbidden books on the sly and meeting with revolutionaries at night, Joseph could not continue his double life at the seminary for long. At 19 he was expelled for missing his exams. For the next couple of years he made a living in Tiflis working at its weather station, but his real energies were poured into another goal—revolution.

Joseph spent his twenties on the move. He soon left his job for the life of a political agitator—stirring up workers to strike, publishing revolutionary broadsheets, always on the run from the authorities. The record of these years is shadowy, but Joseph clearly used this time learning how to organize people for action.

This troublemaker created enough of a stir to be invited in 1905 to a conference of Communists—followers of Marx who wanted to transform Russia into a classless society. Exiled by the czar for their ideas, they had to meet outside the country, this time in Finland. For Stalin, it was a chance to see the revolutionary leader he had heard so much about: Vladimir Ilyich Lenin. Although living and writing in exile, Lenin was keen to direct the progress of Russia's Communist cause from a distance.

Joseph was impressed by Lenin's confidence and charisma. But all the same, he was disappointed to see his hero up close. Joseph had imagined Lenin would be a giant of a leader. Instead he was ordinary-looking and, worse in Joseph's eyes, too informal. Lenin simply did not behave the way Joseph thought a great man should. He should have arrived late, Joseph thought, making his followers wait. "Then, just before the great man enters," Joseph described to a friend, "the warning goes up: 'Hush! Silence! He's coming!'" In Joseph's view, Lenin was breaking "certain essential rules" of leadership.

Few of the sophisticated writers and academics at the conference paid much attention to Joseph, a stocky young man with a thick Georgian accent and shabby clothes. Those who did notice him remembered his pockmarked face and yellow eyes that glinted with hostility. But Lenin saw something more in Joseph. This young recruit might be rough around the edges, Lenin thought, but his results back home with the workers were impressive. Unlike many well-educated party members, here was someone who would likely accept Lenin's instructions and put his plans into action. What Lenin wanted was a small, disciplined party of professional revolutionaries who would seize power on behalf of the workers and peasants.

Lenin's plans seem to have included armed robbery to fund the revolutionary cause. Joseph is said to have planned a bank robbery in Tiflis in 1907, probably on Lenin's instructions. Two carriages loaded with money and escorted by soldiers on horseback were on their way to the State Bank when Joseph's gang raided the convoy. Bombs thrown in the attack killed and injured several people. In smuggling the money out of the country to Lenin, most of the couriers were arrested.

Joseph managed to disappear, avoiding capture. He traveled south to Baku, a port on the Caspian Sea. Its smoky harbor and streets were dominated by oil refineries—and hordes of oil workers from across Russia. Joseph began publishing a union newspaper, *The Baku Proletarian*. Although he never wrote brilliantly, he could put Marx's ideas across in simple, strong terms that uneducated people could understand. He urged the 50,000 oil workers to band together in one big trade union to demand representation in government. The authorities soon arrested him, but he escaped and hid in one of Baku's oil fields.

Soon he was urging the same workers to bring the oil fields to a halt with a general strike. "Two years of revolutionary work among the oil workers of Baku hardened me as a practical fighter ..." he later said. "I first learned what it meant to lead large masses of workers." Time after time Joseph was arrested and exiled to remote areas of the country, but he kept escaping to pick up where he left off.

It was during his restless years on the run that Joseph met the sister of one of his old schoolmates. Ekaterina Svanidze was a quiet, religious girl, and she adored Joseph. As a Marxist, Joseph had rejected religion, but he was so taken with Ekaterina that, to make her happy, he married her in an Orthodox ceremony at a church in Tiflis. Ekaterina was a traditional Georgian wife, and she made their home a safe haven for her revolutionary husband. During his long absences she would pray along with Joseph's mother that he would give up revolution and settle down. Their son, Yakov, was born in 1907. Six months later Ekaterina died. The baby was given to her sister to care for, and Joseph would not see him again for many years.

Joseph's comrades rarely saw him show emotion, but he confided to a friend at Ekaterina's funeral how deeply hurt he was. "This creature softened my stony heart," he said, pointing at her coffin. "She is dead and with her have died my last warm feelings for all human beings."

STALIN: FACTS

Born: December 21, 1879 (official date)
Died: March 5, 1953
Name at birth: Joseph Vissarionovich Dzhugashvili
Titles in power: General Secretary of the Communist Party of the Soviet Union, 1922–53; Premier of the Soviet state, 1941–53; Generalissimo, 1945
Age upon coming to power: 42
Time in power: 31 years
Size of domain: largest country in the world, from eastern Europe to north Asia and the Pacific Ocean, from the Arctic Ocean south to China
Armed forces commanded: Red Army, 12.5 million Russians at its peak in World War II
Number of victims: Historians estimate 20 million.
Defining characteristics: suspicious, secretive, manipulative, revengeful
Legacy: Changed the course of Communism in Russia. Industrialized and modernized the country. Defeated Hitler's armies and made the Soviet Union a world power.

"In this accursed region, nature is stark and ugly: the river in summer, the snow in winter … That's all the scenery there is around here. So I have an idiotic longing to see some landscape, if only on paper." In his letter to friends who had sent him a parcel, Joseph asked for postcards next time—anything to brighten his bleak Siberian surroundings.

In 1913, Joseph was arrested and exiled again, this time to the most remote settlements of Siberia. North of the Arctic Circle, six weeks by sled to the nearest railway, it was a frozen wasteland where the temperature could drop below minus 40°C (-40°F). Security was loose, but the isolation made escape impossible. Exiles had to scrounge for money and food, counting on handouts sent from friends. Joseph learned to hunt and fish in order to eat. He read to help pass the long winter nights.

During this time, arguments were splitting the Communist Party in two. Lenin was now leader of the radical members, the Bolsheviks. His faction was in a showdown with the moderate Mensheviks. Lenin was building up a base loyal to him, and he promoted the absent Joseph to his Central Committee. For Joseph this was an honor: he was now part of Lenin's inner circle.

In 1916, Joseph was allowed to resettle in south-central Russia. With him was another formerly exiled revolutionary, a journalist named Lev Kamenev. There, in 1917, incredible news reached them: the czar had given up his throne. Joseph and Kamenev rushed to the capital, Petrograd, where a provisional government had been formed. The Revolution had started!

As members of Lenin's Central Committee, Joseph and Kamenev wasted no time taking over the Bolshevik newspaper *Pravda*, or "Truth." They wanted to rally

THE RUSSIAN REVOLUTION: A TIMELINE

This violent uprising overthrew Russia's czar, and brought Lenin and Stalin's Bolsheviks into power.

1905
Russia is ruled by a czar. Many are unhappy with the regime's harshness and refusal to share power.

January: A group of workers march to the Winter Palace to petition Czar Nicholas II. Troops fire on the crowd. Riots and strikes follow. The czar agrees to increase citizens' power by creating an elected council called the Duma.

1914
Russia enters World War I.

1917
February: During a general strike in the capital, Petrograd, the czar orders troops to break up the crowds. The soldiers fire on the strikers, but later the garrison mutinies and joins the demonstrators. The czar dissolves the Duma, which refuses to obey. The rebels take over the capital.

March: The Duma appoints a provisional government, whose members are moderate. The czar abdicates.

April: Lenin returns from exile in Switzerland.

October: Lenin's Bolsheviks seize power by force, storming the Winter Palace and government buildings in Petrograd. They form the Council of People's Commissars.

1918
March: The new government negotiates a peace with Germany and withdraws from the war. The ruling party changes its name to the All-Russian Communist Party.

July: The czar and his family are executed.

1918–1920
Civil war breaks out between the new Communist government ("Reds") and anti-Communists ("Whites"). The White Russians are defeated, but not before the country is devastated by the war.

1922
The Union of Soviet Socialist Republics (USSR) is formed.

their supporters while they waited for Lenin, who could now return from exile. The party needed to look strong, Joseph believed. By this time he had dropped his difficult Georgian surname and renamed himself— Stalin, "man of steel."

Lenin's Bolsheviks took over the country in a violent coup in 1917. The Communists were in power at last. But a handful of party members had resisted the action. Lev Kamenev and one of Lenin's closest advisers, Grigorii Zinoviev, opposed seizing power and rejected one-party control of the country. They had imagined a period of co-operation among Russia's parties to run the new government. Zinoviev protested that Lenin's actions were "against the will of the vast majority of workers and soldiers."

Stalin, as usual, remained quiet on the matter. In fact, those who later tried to remember Stalin from the party congresses of this time had trouble doing so. He was, they said, more like a "gray blur." Smoking his pipe, wearing his peasant's tunic and heavy boots, he seldom spoke out. When he did, it was quietly, in small groups. More often he listened, expressing no opinion while others debated. Then he would sum up according to whichever way the argument was drifting. He took pains to sound reasonable and avoid extreme statements. He still spoke in the plain language of a party worker from the provinces.

Most important, he kept impressing Lenin as a man who could get things done. This reputation scored him the position of General Secretary to the party in 1922. It was a job created to organize all the complex tasks the party faced now that it was in power. Stalin had his own reasons for taking on the unglamorous job. He used his new post to find out about everything and everyone in the party. Slowly, he was also taking control of the party's various branches—without ever drawing attention to himself. Soon Stalin was hand-picking people for key positions on every rung of the party ladder—people who would later owe their positions to him.

Lenin appreciated his efficient right-hand man. No one guessed how dangerous it was to put so much control in Stalin's hands. Comrade Stalin might be rude to other party members, and he didn't seem brainy enough to decide party policy—but dangerous? There had as yet been no evidence of Stalin's ruthlessness. Stalin was also careful to keep quiet about his own ambition—which was to be Lenin's successor. Stalin did not mind being underestimated for the time being. He knew he was no charismatic speaker or revolutionary hero. That was a role being played by another party member: Leon Trotsky.

Stalin and Trotsky were like day and night. From their first encounter, in 1913 in Vienna, their differences were obvious. Trotsky was an impressive man to meet. Tall and striking, he was an excellent speaker, well traveled, and intellectual. Stalin was his opposite in almost every way: short, rough-looking, and untalkative. He was uneasy around well-educated people and distrusted them.

Stalin quickly grasped that the greatest obstacle to his ambitions was Trotsky. He had flaws but was a natural leader with huge popular appeal, someone who was often greeted with a standing ovation when he walked into the party congress. While Trotsky was becoming a public hero, Stalin kept up his usual work behind the scenes. But he never took his eyes off his rival. Trotsky, on the other hand, was too self-confident to pay attention to the party secretary—until it was too late.

"Comrade Stalin, having become General Secretary, has concentrated limitless power in his hands, and I am not sure that he will always manage to use this power with sufficient caution ..." It was 1923, and Lenin was dying. A stroke had confined him to his apartment in Moscow's Kremlin. His doctor had tried to keep him from working, but Lenin insisted on writing in his diary. In fact he was secretly composing a final message to the next party congress, which he might not live to see. Lenin was concerned that the government had strayed too far from the cause of the workers, and worried that too much power was concentrated in too few hands. Most of all, he was alarmed by the prospect of leaving Stalin in control.

Almost too late, Lenin had recognized the threat Stalin posed. Now he could see that he had relied for too long on Stalin's efficiency, overlooking the gruff way he brushed aside other comrades. In his message Lenin summed up the strengths and weaknesses of the party members. He singled out Leon Trotsky for praise. Several days later, Lenin added a postscript to his message that was much more direct: remove Stalin. "Find a way to transfer Stalin," he wrote, "... and appoint another man more tolerant, more loyal, more polite, and more considerate of comrades ..." Lenin sealed the letter and put it into the hands of his wife.

When Lenin died in January 1924, Stalin seized the moment. He had already taken advantage of Trotsky's absences due to illness to discredit him or squeeze him out of decision making. Now he cabled Trotsky, giving him the wrong date for Lenin's funeral. Trotsky was not among the mourners, and it damaged his reputation. Stalin was there and played his part well. He helped carry Lenin's coffin. In a speech, he promised to fulfill Lenin's "commandments." He did everything to pose as the guardian of Lenin's legacy.

Then, just before the party congress, Lenin's widow brought her husband's final testament to a small meeting of the Central Committee. Before this inner circle, she insisted that Lenin's last words be read before the whole party at the congress—and that Lenin's dying wish to remove Stalin be carried out. Stalin, sitting slightly apart, remained silent and stared out the window. He was trying hard to appear unconcerned, although his fate was being decided.

During Lenin's illness, Stalin had decided matters with the help of Lev Kamenev and Grigorii Zinoviev. They were not all friends, but a common enemy united them: Trotsky. History showed that revolutions could end with a dictator taking power, and Kamenev and Zinoviev agreed that the charismatic Trotsky might pose such a danger. Now, Stalin waited quietly for their reaction to Lenin's letter. Zinoviev spoke up first. Lenin's fears about Stalin had turned out to be wrong, he declared. Kamenev argued that Stalin should keep his job. Both urged that Lenin's testament not be read aloud to the congress. They were successful, and Lenin's dying wishes would remain secret until the 1950s.

Stalin breathed a sigh of relief. Luckily for him, his rivals continued to underestimate him and his ambitions. They also remained too suspicious of one another to unite against him. Years later, when Lenin's wife spoke out again over something else dear to Lenin's heart,

Stalin would be in a position to issue a sinister warning. "Tell her we can always find someone else to be Lenin's widow," he said.

During the Communists' rise to power, Stalin had married again, this time the daughter of one of his revolutionary comrades. More than 20 years younger than Stalin, Nadezhda Allilueva was a devoted Communist and in awe of her important husband. She soon had a son, Vasily, followed by a girl, Svetlana. In 1922, Stalin summoned his son from his first marriage to live with his new family in Moscow's Kremlin. Yakov was now 15 and about to get to know his father for the first time. But Stalin never accepted him. Yakov's thick Georgian accent embarrassed Stalin, who wanted to distance himself from his roots. The boy's slow progress at school irritated him, and Stalin sometimes lashed out at Yakov as his father had done to him.

Stalin was soon spending little time at home with his family, as party politics took up all his hours. A showdown with Trotsky was coming, and it would be fought over an issue that had long divided Communists. Should their aim be uniting workers everywhere in a worldwide revolution—as Lenin had pictured—or should they focus on "socialism in one country"? That meant rebuilding Russia, which had been torn by war and revolution. Trotsky, the idealist, promoted the cause of workers worldwide engaging in an ongoing revolution. Kamenev and Zinoviev agreed. But Stalin, a good listener, had a knack for sensing the general mood of the party. People wanted stability after so much war and hardship. Yes, Stalin declared, working to build socialism in one country was possible.

THE SOVIET UNION UNDER STALIN

/// Communist states established after World War II

[ ] The Union of Soviet Socialist Republics (USSR)

Stalin annexed new territory to the already vast Soviet Union during World War II, and by the war's end exerted his control over the Communist states of eastern Europe.

In 1927, Stalin won the battle. Trotsky was expelled from the Central Committee. With him went Kamenev and Zinoviev, who had helped Stalin weather the storm of Lenin's final testament. Rejected by the party, Trotsky was exiled from the Soviet Union in 1929. Stalin was now Lenin's undisputed successor. But even that did not completely satisfy him. In 1940, Stalin would send assassins to Mexico to murder Trotsky, and he would continue to smear his name long after his death.

Across the Russian countryside, smoke from burning crops blackened the sky. Farmhouses stood abandoned. Slaughtered herds of animals lay in the barns and fields. It looked like a land ravaged by war—but Russia was not at war. "Land to the peasants!" the Bolsheviks had promised in 1917. Now the peasants' dream of owning their own land had turned into a nightmare.

A single death is a tragedy; a million deaths is a statistic.
—Stalin

Stalin was determined to modernize Russia's industries and agriculture by storm. His first goal was to bring every farm under government control. Peasants would work together on huge state-owned farms called collectives. The state would own and distribute all the grain and food that was farmed.

But Russia's peasants were known to be traditionalists who resisted change. They worked their plots of land in isolated communities, far from the city-dwellers who ran the government. Lenin had predicted it would take a decade or two before they could be convinced to band together on the new collective farms. The poorest peasants, who owned no land, would likely volunteer to join the collectives, but land-owning farmers would resist giving up their independence, Lenin said. They should be encouraged to do so with rewards, he had suggested. But Stalin was too impatient to wait. A second revolution was needed to complete Lenin's work, he felt. And this time, Stalin said, it would be a "revolution from above."

In 1930, brigades of party workers and soldiers spread through the countryside. They dragged peasants off their farms at gunpoint. Harvests, livestock, and equipment were carted away to the new collectives. But well-off farmers, called kulaks, were not wanted; they

In this government photo, farmers on a collective head out to the fields while agents from an official newspaper set up nearby. The reality of the collectives was very different: peasants suffered extreme hardship and starvation.

were "class enemies." Kulak families were herded onto cattle wagons and transported to Siberia. There, millions were either abandoned or packed into work camps. In protest, desperate peasants began smashing their own farming equipment and slaughtering their livestock rather than hand them over to the collectives.

Stalin refused to slow the pace, but he did try to distance himself from the harsh measures. In *Pravda* he attacked the local officials who were carrying out collectivization. "Collective farms cannot be set up by force," he declared. "To do so would be stupid." He blamed his agents for twisting his directives. For many peasants, this propaganda ploy worked.

Their faith in Stalin was soon put to the hardest test of all. A famine gripped Russia in 1932, beginning in the Ukraine. Drought started it, but Stalin's orders to keep taking grain from the farms—including the grain needed to plant the next year's harvest—turned it into an epic disaster. The state's reserves of grain were kept from the starving masses. Watchtowers were built around the crops to keep hungry peasants from stealing food. The sentence for taking a handful of grain was 10 years' labor, or death. By early 1933, more than 50,000 people had been convicted. Millions more survived only by farming a tiny plot of land on the side.

Stalin took a distant view of the peasants' suffering and refused to admit there was a famine. There were only some "difficulties and shortages" in the countryside, he said. Stalin was determined to keep news of the farmers' situation from reaching other countries; no one must know that his second revolution was a disaster. Roadblocks prevented peasants from leaving their land, and newspapers were forbidden to report the famine; mentioning it was punished with five years' hard labor.

The last time famine had struck Russia, the Bolsheviks had asked for international aid, but Stalin refused to show weakness by doing the same.

In the end, 25 million farms were turned into a quarter-million collectives. As many as 14.5 million people died in the process. Stalin's "war against the peasants" killed more people than had died from all countries in World War I.

Stalin had not forgotten the cities in his plans. The world was entering the age of the machine, and he did not want Russia to be left behind. In 1928, he announced his first "five-year plan"—setting astonishing targets for oil, coal, and steel production. Stalin tackled this goal with the same impatience he had shown with the collectives. "It is sometimes asked whether it is not possible to slow down the tempo a bit," he told the party congress. "No, comrades, it is not possible! We are fifty or a hundred years behind the advanced countries. We must make good this distance in ten years. Either we do it, or they crush us."

To keep up this furious pace, industrial workers were forbidden to change jobs, take days off, or be late; these were now crimes that carried stiff prison sentences. No one would say publicly that the objectives were unrealistic. Factory managers learned to lie about how much they were producing.

Stalin's wife, Nadezhda, was alarmed by the changes in her husband. She had lately watched him become crueler, colder. In 1932, she committed suicide. Stalin was shaken and baffled. But he did not alter his path in the least.

After Nadezhda's death, Stalin grew distant from

Men and women at a factory strive to meet the production goals set by Stalin's five-year plan.

his sons. When he did see them, he bullied and dominated them. Only one person received any affection from him, his daughter Svetlana. Stalin called her his "little housekeeper" and treated her with a gruff tenderness. All that changed when Svetlana became a teenager, however. Stalin became stern, insisting that she wear long, old-fashioned skirts. When she began dating an older man, he ordered agents to follow the couple and to record their telephone conversations.

By this time Stalin's suspiciousness was beginning to show itself in disturbing ways—and it did not stop at his family.

A trial was in progress in August 1936. Accused of treason, 16 men stood before three judges. Foreign journalists and diplomats had been allowed in the courtroom, and 150 Soviet citizens sat in the audience. The state prosecutor questioned the accused, going over their confessions. "I demand that these mad dogs be shot, every last one of them!" he declared.

The whole event was a sham, a show trial put on for the benefit of the Russian public and any party members who might consider disagreeing with Stalin. The audience was mostly staff of the NKVD— Stalin's secret police—waiting for their cue to voice an uproar of disapproval against the defendants. The "confessions" had been obtained by force, and the accused were reminded that their families' lives depended on them giving the expected answers in court. Stalin had already approved their sentences— before a word of the trial had been heard.

There are internal enemies, comrades. There are external enemies. This is never to be forgotten.
—Stalin

Two of the men in the dock were Stalin's old comrades Kamenev and Zinoviev. They were accused of conspiring with others to assassinate a party leader named Sergei Kirov. The supposed ringleader of this conspiracy was none other than the exiled Trotsky.

In fact it may have been Stalin himself who ordered the murder of Kirov, who was too popular in the party for Stalin's liking. In any case, he took advantage of the event. He praised the dead Kirov as a revolutionary hero, then set about hunting down his "assassins." Investigators uncovered a web of "conspirators" that included everyone Stalin considered a threat. Stalin had always feared that others within the party might plot to overthrow him, and his suspicions turned the NKVD investigations into massive purges. The doomed suspects were accused of crimes such as sabotage, weakening the Red Army, spying for foreign enemies, even trying to restore capitalism. While Stalin must have known the accusations were lies, the suspects *were* guilty of something in his mind: standing between him and absolute control. Between 1936 and 1939 more than half of the party was arrested.

Citizens began pointing their fingers at others out of fear, just to prove they were loyal. Officials felt pressured to discover "traitors" among their ranks. Neighbors

ERASING HISTORY

Wherever the past was inconvenient to recall, Stalin did not hesitate to change it. He had the images of Trotsky and Kamenev removed from photos showing them with Lenin. Students were told to tear pages out of their history texts or paste new versions overtop. The new accounts glorified Stalin's role in the Revolution and revised the actions of his enemies to justify their executions.

Stalin tinkered with a story close to revolutionaries' hearts: the faithful Bolsheviks meeting Lenin upon his return to Russia in 1917. No one bothered to record whether Stalin was there or not, and at the time Lenin was annoyed by the recent actions of party members. Stalin had the episode rewritten. Now history books told of a joyful reunion between Stalin and Lenin, the two "great leaders" embracing on the train platform.

People were told what to think about the present too. An official slogan broadcast in 1935, during the terror and show trials, proclaimed: "Life has become better, comrades; life has become more joyous."

denounced neighbors; students denounced teachers; workers denounced factory managers. Children were taught to be suspicious of their parents and to stay on guard for any comments against the party. Sometimes whole groups were targeted. "Class enemies" who had been privileged before the Revolution or had voiced opposition within the party were rounded up, as were scientists, writers, and scholars.

Suspects were awakened in the middle of the night by loud knocks on the door. NKVD men searched the apartment, took papers, then marched the arrested

A gap grew between the reality citizens could see around them and the "truth" dictated by the party. For many people, life under Stalin meant endless lineups for basic necessities, families crowded into one-room apartments, shabby clothes, inadequate food, and long work hours to meet impossible targets. But to talk about these things was out of the question. As comrade Stalin insisted in 1933, "We have without doubt achieved a situation in which the material conditions of workers and peasants are improving year by year. The only people who doubt this are the sworn enemies of Soviet power."

The full number of people executed or exiled by Stalin would be revealed only decades later, when the Soviet government adopted a policy of *glasnost*—"openness"—and with the fall of Communism in the early 1990s. Many crimes were made public at last. Some who had lived through the era were upset by the news. At the time they had really believed they were working for a better socialist future. In Russia's recent troubled times a few have even idealized Stalin as the strong leader who made their country a world power.

person outside to a waiting car. The victim's family were immediately shunned by neighbors and friends; any further contact with them was too dangerous. Those taken into custody were interrogated, sometimes tortured, until they confessed to false accusations. Some were sent to gulags—the labor camps Stalin had installed across Siberia. Many were executed.

The purges spread to the Red Army as well. By the end of the 1930s, at least 35,000 officers—about half of the entire corps—had been executed or imprisoned. In his hurry to weed out his enemies, Stalin had left the country exposed to attack. And war was on the horizon—with Germany's Adolf Hitler.

Germany's dictator was the enemy of everything Communism stood for. And yet, in 1939, Stalin signed a pact with Adolf Hitler: the two countries promised not to wage war against each other. Stalin had watched Hitler take steps to expand his empire, and he did not trust England or France to stand against him. Stalin decided to delay a war with Germany for as long as possible, at least until he had rebuilt the ruined Red Army.

Then Germany launched a surprise invasion. In June 1941, more than 3 million German troops swept across the Russian border. Divisions of German tanks met little resistance from the weakened Red Army. The Russian air force was destroyed while still on the ground. Stalin's harsh treatment of his own people also helped the enemy: in some areas the Germans were welcomed at first as liberators. In the first six months, the enemy captured 3 million Russian soldiers—65 percent of the Soviet armed forces.

Stalin was stunned by his miscalculation. Britain

had warned him of the coming invasion, but he so little trusted the English that he ignored them. He had even ordered his commanders guarding the border not to do anything to provoke the Germans. For two weeks after the invasion Stalin froze in the face of the disaster. He retreated to his dacha, a summer cottage, where he read a play about Ivan the Terrible. In his absence the government set up a State Committee of Defense, but its members were too frightened to issue orders without Stalin's signature. They drove out to the dacha to beg Stalin to return.

IVAN THE TERRIBLE: A HERO?

Like other tyrants, Stalin used history for his own purposes. He was choosy about which parts of Russia's past he would glorify and which he would conveniently forget. Stalin encouraged writers and filmmakers such as Sergei Eisenstein to remake the image of Ivan the Terrible. Stalin wanted to glorify Ivan as the man who united a strong Russia, who struck down a corrupt aristocracy, and who rewarded common people for their service and loyalty—all accomplishments Stalin was anxious to take credit for in his own time. Ivan's legendary cruelty was downplayed or denied. In the 16th century as in Stalin's era, it was said, the country needed a strong leader who punished evildoers.

Other tyrants have been just as anxious to link themselves with heroes from the past. In posters and speeches Hitler liked to show himself as the heir to German heroes such as Frederick the Great and Bismarck. The mention of these men stirred patriotic feelings in people, and Hitler hoped to tap into this powerful response. Robespierre did the same by comparing himself to the republicans of early Rome, men much admired by French revolutionaries for their selfless dedication to their country.

Stalin looked depressed and exhausted—and puzzled as to why they had come. For a second, fear flashed across his face: were they there to arrest him? He was relieved when they asked him to come back. Stalin agreed.

When he spoke to the nation over the radio, his tone and words surprised everyone. "Comrades, citizens, brothers and sisters, men of our army and navy! It is to you I am speaking, dear friends. Grave danger overhangs our country. The Red Army and all citizens of the Soviet Union must defend every inch of Soviet soil, must fight to the last drop of blood ..." In Stalin's plea to Russians to defend their country, there was not a Communist slogan to be heard. Russians were amazed when the party secretary called them "brothers and sisters"—a traditional Russian greeting unused since the Revolution. Stalin was appealing to their patriotism as Russians, not their obedience as good Communists.

In the months that followed, the old army uniforms and ranks were brought back—even though they had been outlawed in the new classless society. Over 80 percent of the imprisoned Red Army officers were put back into action. The emptied divisions were rapidly supplied with soldiers in any possible way.

Anyone who thought Stalin had become less ruthless quickly learned otherwise. He terrorized his generals into launching counterattacks against the Germans, making sure his army was more afraid of him than of the enemy. "In the Red Army," he said, "it takes more courage to retreat than to advance." Stalin ordered special detachments to follow troops with orders to "shoot the panic-mongers and cowards on the spot." If the army was ordered to retreat, it was to destroy everything in its path, leaving nothing of use for the enemy.

Stalin's ruthlessness extended even to his family. When Yakov, an army lieutenant, was captured by the Germans, Stalin called him a traitor and refused to exchange a prisoner for him. He feared Yakov was weak enough to betray him. Yet in private, Stalin agonized over Yakov's fate, and kept his other son, Vasily, from active duty.

Leningrad, the renamed city of Petrograd, remained under siege by the Germans for two and a half years—the longest siege in history. But it did not surrender. Germany's advance on Moscow was slowed by the fierce Russian winter. Fuel froze in German tanks; soldiers' boots cracked apart. When winter-ready Siberian troops pushed the Germans back, it was a tremendous boost for Russian morale. Moscow had been saved; Stalin did not abandon the city. "Not one step back!" Stalin ordered the garrison defending the city named in his honor—Stalingrad. And this ferocious battle proved to be the turning point of the war.

The streets of Moscow were filled with crowds. Victorious Red Army officers paraded through Red Square, driving before them thousands of ragged German prisoners of war. Watching from the top of Lenin's mausoleum was a triumphant Stalin. Marching briskly, waves of Soviet soldiers mounted the steps of the platform to throw captured German flags at Stalin's feet before turning on their heels and descending.

Stalin's brutal methods had won the Great Patriotic War, but at a staggering cost. One in ten Russians—20 million people—had been killed, hundreds of thousands more were permanently injured. Cities, towns, and villages had been wiped off the map, leaving 25 million

Refugees are herded onto train cars for deportation to labor camps in Siberia. Stalin—who himself spent 8½ years of exile in this cold and isolated region— sent millions of suspected traitors and political enemies to camps there.

people homeless. This dearly bought victory won international prestige for Stalin. At the end of the war he met with the other Allied leaders to draw up the boundaries of post-war Europe. But it soon became clear to the rest of the world that Stalin had liberated much of eastern and southeastern Europe so he could conquer it himself.

Those Russians who hoped victory would mean better times were disappointed. Hundreds of thousands of Russian soldiers returning home were marched straight into labor camps in Siberia. Their contact with the enemy had "contaminated" them. The same fate awaited millions of people who had lived under German occupation. Stalin regarded them all as possible traitors. A new five-year plan was announced: citizens must work harder than ever to make up for the destruction of the war.

Stalin was determined to hide from the world how badly the war had devastated the "powerful" Soviet Union and the low standard of living of its survivors. Strict controls were placed over the movement of people and information into and out of the country. Soon, Stalin had cut the country off from the West. The breakdown of relations between the Soviet Union and the other Allies escalated into a cold war that would last decades. With it would come a terrifying arms race between the two superpowers that emerged from World War II: the Soviet Union and its new arch-enemy, the United States.

Although his image was still everywhere, within a few years of the war Stalin stopped making public appearances. Why tarnish his superhuman reputation by showing his aging? The number of guards surrounding him had grown larger and larger. At night, his home was ringed by troops and dogs. Visitors who had not seen Stalin since the war could not believe how much he had changed. He was no longer as quick-witted, and would often misunderstand a joke and take offense. Yet he remained as stubborn and suspicious as ever.

In his isolation, Stalin relaxed by watching films in his private theater. Other than his daughter and his housekeeper, his only companions were the subordinates forced to attend all-night dinners at his dacha. Stalin ate nothing unless it had been tasted by another for poison. He amused himself by

You are blind, like young kittens. What will happen here without me? The country will perish—you do not know how to recognize an enemy.
—Stalin

THE CULT OF PERSONALITY

While Stalin used mass arrests and executions to rid himself of any opposition in the party, he broadcast a very different image of himself to the public. The nation was flooded with his image in posters, paintings, and statues. Every workplace, school, and home was expected to display his picture as a sign of loyalty. His idealized portraits did not show his pockmarked face or withered left hand. He was depicted as tall and handsome, striding heroically into the future or looking affectionately down over his people. Newspapers, posters, and films celebrated his many roles.

"Stalin is the brilliant leader and teacher of the Party," his official biography stated, "the great strategist of the Socialist Revolution, military commander, the guide of the Soviet state ... Everybody is familiar with the ... invincible force of Stalin's logic, the crystal clarity of his mind, his iron will ... and love for the people ... Stalin is the Lenin of today."

Stalin often sent agents from his security police across the country to listen in on what people were saying about him. "People speak of Stalin's simplicity and accessibility," they reported back. "They say that Stalin is not to blame for the bad things that happen: 'He follows the right line, but around him are scoundrels.'" Stalin was pleased: his image campaign was working!

forcing his guests to get drunk and making them dance. Everyone laughed at his jokes and stories even though they had heard them a hundred times before.

Now in his early seventies, Stalin let his suspicions direct his every move. Without warning he turned on some of his most faithful followers. He ordered the arrests of his doctor along with several other specialists who treated the party elite. They were plotting to kill him and other key party members, Stalin declared. He ordered that confessions be secured from all the doctors by whatever means necessary. Russians braced themselves for the purge to come. How far would Stalin take it this time?

Thankfully, no one ever found out. In 1953, Stalin suffered a stroke. He lay semi-conscious for three and a half days, then died. One by one the party members surrounding his bedside rushed out the door to their limousines, each one terrified of being left behind in the struggle for power that would follow. A party mourner at Stalin's funeral joked, "Today the mice have buried the cat." And yet throughout Russia people reacted to Stalin's death with shock and fear. Many cried. He had controlled every part of their lives for 25 years. How could they imagine life without him?

Stalin's place would be taken by Nikita Khrushchev. This long-time party member would reveal many of the crimes of Stalin's regime and release thousands of gulag prisoners. He would also, in his aggressive stance towards the United States, bring the world to the brink of nuclear war.

SADDAM HUSSEIN
THE STRONGMAN OF BAGHDAD

Iraq, 1991

"The great, the jewel, and the mother of all battles has begun."

In a radio broadcast, Iraq's president, Saddam Hussein, told his people that they were at war. Just where or when he had recorded the statement, or if it was a live speech, was unknown. But Saddam Hussein often kept his location a secret.

The 53-year-old president had gambled boldly in August 1990 by sending his army across the border into Kuwait, a small Arab country on the coast of the Persian Gulf. Saddam wagered that other countries would not interfere, and his Iraqi force of 120,000 troops overran Kuwait easily. Many soldiers from Kuwait's small army were killed or captured. Then Iraqi troops moved south towards the Saudi Arabian border. Would that country be next?

The United Nations demanded that Iraq withdraw its troops from Kuwait. The United States halted exports to Iraq. Days later, the UN voted to enforce an international embargo; countries belonging to the UN would no longer buy Iraq's oil. But Saddam Hussein was defiant as a coalition force of more than 60,000 soldiers from a variety of countries gathered in Saudi Arabia, where they prepared to repel the Iraqi invaders.

A Kuwaiti engineer warned the coalition that Iraqi troops had planted mines on a third of Kuwait's oil wells. If the mines exploded during an attack, the burning oil could do enormous damage to the environment. The possibilities were frightening: mass illness, crop destruction, poisoned drinking water, even an increase in global warming. The coalition troops would have to seize the oil fields quickly. At the same time, the people of Iraq braced themselves for the air attacks that would soon hit their country.

Iraq had not yet recovered from the eight-year war with Iran that Saddam Hussein had started in 1980, believing then too that an easy conquest could be made. What kind of man would be so reckless as to bring the Iraqi people to the brink of destruction again?

As a child, Saddam Hussein's life was shaped by two things: poverty at home and conflict throughout his country. Iraq had long been controlled by other powerful nations. Following World War I, Britain had governed the area. By 1932, Iraq was officially independent and ruled by a king, but British control lingered. Resentment grew among Iraqis who were Arab nationalists. They despised their king for letting the British dominate them.

For many other Iraqis, however, Arab independence was not the main concern. Most of the population lived in poor farming and shepherding communities. Their loyalties were to their family and their village. It was in one of these small villages, al-Shawish, that Saddam Hussein grew up.

Life in al-Shawish was harsh. People lived in mud-brick houses without running water or electricity. Poor nutrition claimed the lives of many young children. Those who reached their teens often joined gangs. By the age of nine, Saddam had started carrying an iron bar to protect himself. The other village boys teased him because he had no father and because his mother's new husband, nicknamed "Hassan the liar," was a known thief. The name Saddam's mother had chosen for him, which meant "He who confronts," had turned out to be a perfect fit. Saddam learned to stay alert and to act tougher than he felt.

Saddam's stepfather beat him and kept the boy out of school to steal for him. Before moving in with Hassan, Saddam had lived in Tikrit with his uncle, Khairallah Tulfah, an army officer. Saddam idolized him and dreamed of going back there.

THE WORLD OF IRAQ

Iraq lies in a part of the world known as "the cradle of civilization." The people of Mesopotamia, now modern Iraq, may have been the first to plant crops, use calendars, and invent a written alphabet—around 4000 BCE.

For centuries, the area that would later become Iraq was a trio of provinces dominated by Turkey's Ottoman Empire. After Turkey's defeat in World War I, the new state of Iraq was created, under British protection and control. But Iraq's first king had little hope of unifying his subjects. Then as now, Iraq was home to different groups who often opposed one another.

The majority of Iraqis are Shia Muslims, living mostly in the south, but under Saddam Hussein the minority Sunni Muslims held the power. To the north live the Kurds, a fiercely independent group. These divisions make Iraq "one of the most difficult nations in the world to govern," according to Saddam's former chief of intelligence. Saddam would later justify his harsh regime by arguing that a divided people needed a strong leader. And only a strong leader could stand up to Western powers and promote Arab interests.

Khairallah was a passionate Arab nationalist. During World War II he had worked for a Nazi victory. If Britain lost to the Germans, he had hoped, it would be thrown out of Iraq once and for all. Khairallah took part in an uprising against a British air base in Iraq. Defeated, he was thrown out of the army and imprisoned.

When Saddam turned 10, his dream came true. His uncle was released from prison and Saddam returned to live with him. He soaked up his uncle's ideas like a sponge: a love of the military and the dream of a united Arab world. Khairallah taught Saddam never to back down from an enemy, no matter how strong. The boy drank in his uncle's prejudices too. Years later, Saddam would order the state press to publish Khairallah's writings, which revealed a deep hostility towards Jews and Persians (Iranians).

When Khairallah moved to Baghdad, the capital of Iraq, 18-year-old Saddam went with him. Wanting to follow in his uncle's footsteps, Saddam applied to the Baghdad Military Academy. But his poor schooling held him back; at 10, he had still been unable to write his own name. Saddam failed the academy entrance exams. It was a heavy blow.

In Baghdad, Saddam found a city on the verge of revolution. Its coffee houses and shops were full of angry talk about the country's pro-Western monarchy. In 1956, talk boiled over into riots in the streets. Saddam had started high school, but the excitement of revolutionary activities was more tempting. He joined the Baath Party.

At first a secret anti-British group, the Baath ("Resurrection") Party was one of several groups preaching unity and independence for Arabs. The Baathists assigned Saddam to lure students at his high school into anti-government actions. Saddam, now a tall, strong young man, tackled this job with energy. He organized gangs of students and local thugs to beat up political opponents and intimidate people in his Baghdad suburb.

The Baathists were overjoyed when, in 1958, a group of army officers toppled the monarchy. But they were not satisfied for long. Once the military installed General Qassem as dictator, it was hard to tell the difference between the new regime and the old one. Qassem refused to form a closer union with other Arab nations, as the Baathists wanted, and the Baathists found themselves shut out of decision making.

In October 1959, Saddam was given his most dangerous assignment yet. He and three other gunmen were to lie in wait for a car carrying President Qassem home from his office. If the gunmen were successful, the car would never get there. Saddam's job was to protect the assassins while they attacked their target. But when the car came into view, Saddam started firing too soon. His partners hesitated, giving Qassem's bodyguards precious time to respond to the attack. The president was wounded, but still alive. Saddam, shot in the leg, escaped.

President Qassem ordered the arrest of all Baath Party members. Saddam fled to Syria, then Egypt. The botched assassination had taught him important lessons about self-control and patience. In Egypt, Saddam at last finished high school at the age of 24. He then studied law, but did not graduate. While in Egypt, Saddam also decided to marry. To strengthen the ties to his clan, he chose his uncle's daughter, Sajidah Tulfah.

IRAQ AND THE MIDDLE EAST

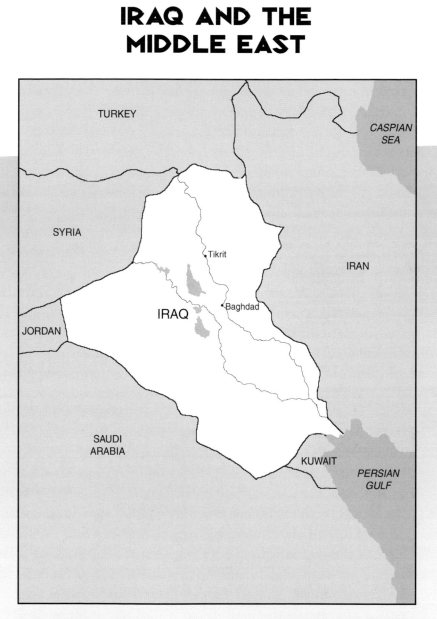

In his quest to make Iraq a dominant power in the Middle East, Saddam Hussein waged a disastrous war against Iran from 1980 to 1988 and invaded Kuwait in 1990.

Saddam wrote home to arrange the match and the couple became engaged.

In 1963, Saddam was thrilled to learn of another coup in Iraq; the Baathists and a group of military officers had seized power. He hurried back from Egypt, but discovered that his time away had reduced his standing in the party. He was now a low-ranking member, shut out of the powerful inner circle. To climb up, he knew he needed allies. Family connections were the key, Saddam believed. He placed himself at the service of his cousin from Tikrit, a Baathist officer named Ahmad Hasan al-Bakr.

Then, with alarming speed, the Baathists were thrown out of the government in a double-cross by the military they had helped into power. Baath members again found themselves on the run from arrest. Saddam faced a choice: he could escape to Syria—and possibly be called a coward if the party's luck improved—or he could stay and risk arrest. After thinking it over carefully, Saddam decided to stay. At worst, he would get a prison term, and he would look like a martyr for the Baath cause.

Saddam was arrested and sentenced to two years in prison, time he used well. He dominated the other Baathists in jail, becoming their unofficial leader. Saddam's wife and baby son, Uday, visited him weekly, and he used these meetings to stay in touch with his ally al-Bakr, hiding messages in Uday's clothes.

Saddam would have to wait until 1968 for the Baathists to join forces with senior officers in yet another coup. Help from two of the officers came with a price: they wanted to be the premier and minister of defense in the new regime. The Baathists agreed. But they had no intention of making the same mistake again. This time they would dispose of their military accomplices before the Baathists themselves could be pushed out of power. Saddam agreed wholeheartedly with this strategy.

The Baath leaders quickly set up the Revolutionary Command Council as Iraq's supreme authority. General al-Bakr became its president and rewarded Saddam's loyalty by appointing Saddam, now 31, vice-president. Not a month had passed before the officers who had helped the Baathists were forced out of the country.

The new regime wasted no time in securing its position. Among Saddam's responsibilities was security, and he led the first of many purges. In Saddam's mind, only force and the show of force could keep him and his allies in power. So-called traitors and spies were hanged in public to set an example. It became a crime punishable by death to belong to an opposition party. People in the new Iraq were required to show patriotism, a love of hard work, and, above all, unity. "We must ensure that the thirteen and a half million [Iraqis] take the same road," Saddam declared. "He who chooses the twisted path will meet the sword."

Together, al-Bakr and Saddam ran the government. Al-Bakr brought support from the military and a reputation as an Arab nationalist. Saddam offered his ability to work long hours behind the scenes. He had already shown a ruthless streak by taking charge of interrogations—and torture—of suspected spies and party opponents. He also saw to it that the party recruited its own militia of 50,000 troops. They looked to Saddam for their orders and provided a safeguard against the powerful army.

Saddam had never forgotten his rejection by the military, but the power he now wielded would help hide the wound, if not heal it: al-Bakr made him a general. Saddam took care of his lack of education in a similar way: he arranged to have a law degree and a Master of Military Science given to him.

Al-Bakr handed over more and more responsibility to his right-hand man. The list of Saddam's roles grew. In addition to security, he took on education and propaganda. The president made the announcements and signed decrees, while Saddam stood respectfully behind him in public. But it was soon known that Saddam— now nicknamed "the strongman of Baghdad"—exercised the real power in the government.

Saddam Hussein was not willing to remain al-Bakr's second-in-command forever. The president was elderly, and Saddam suspected he was growing out of touch; he might get in the way of the harsh actions Saddam used to stay in control. Worse, Saddam feared the old general might squeeze him out as his successor at the last minute. The time had come, Saddam decided, to take charge.

Al-Bakr knew better than to resist. In July 1979, he announced on Iraqi television that he was stepping down because of health problems. He praised Saddam as a "brilliant leader." Saddam was poised to step into his shoes. Not so fast, objected some party leaders. They called for a party vote to elect the new president.

Saddam responded quickly and ruthlessly. Later the same month, he invited the Revolutionary Command Council and party leaders to a Baghdad conference hall. After a low-key start to the proceedings, Saddam strode to the podium. The words he spoke into the microphone sent a shiver down his listeners' spines. There had been a betrayal, a plot, Saddam said slowly, within the party itself. On cue, the secretary-general of the RCC was brought forward to confess. Saddam's interrogators had tortured the man and drilled a speech into him in advance. Obediently, the secretary-general gave the names of his fellow plotters—all of them sitting in the audience.

Guards escorted the accused men out one by one as their names were spoken. Saddam took a seat to the side, calmly smoking a cigar. A man protested that he was innocent. "Get out!" Saddam snapped. He decided to have the men's mouths taped shut on the way to their executions, so they couldn't speak any damaging last words.

The frightening show in the conference hall sent a clear message. There would be no election; Saddam alone was in charge. His audience understood. When the arrests ended, those left behind stood and applauded. "Long live Saddam!" they began to chant. Some even called for more traitors to be exposed.

In the days that followed, videotapes of the event were sent to other party officials, to make sure everyone was intimidated. People on the streets of Baghdad got the same message from the six-meter (20-foot) posters of Saddam Hussein that were quickly plastered onto walls.

Saddam was at last in complete control, but he knew he could not afford to loosen his grip. Force and deceit had helped him climb to the top, and he knew better than anyone that a coup could topple him. Since his childhood, he had believed that the world was a cruel place full of ruthless, cunning enemies. But Saddam felt confident that he had an advantage: he was even more ruthless and cunning. "I know that there are scores of people plotting to kill me," Saddam admitted to a guest shortly after becoming president. "After all, did we not seize power by plotting against our predecessors? However, I am far cleverer than they are. I know they are conspiring to kill me long before they actually start planning to do it. This enables me to get them before they have the faintest chance of striking at me."

Among his first actions was another purge of government officials he suspected of disloyalty, some of them old friends. He also doubled the ranks of the party's private army. The new president made sure the government was dominated by kinsmen from Tikrit, the only people Saddam trusted. "You need the family to protect you, not an army or a party," Saddam's uncle Khairallah often said. "Armies and parties change direction in this country." Khairallah's son was made minister of defense. Khairallah himself became mayor of Baghdad, and was soon known for his greed and corruption. All of Saddam's relatives began to drop his name to get whatever they wanted.

To secure his power, the new president looked to strongmen of the past for role models. A politician visiting Saddam in 1979 was disturbed to find that all the books in Saddam's office were on one subject: Joseph Stalin. Saddam certainly matched the Soviet tyrant's tactics step by step on his climb to power: working his way up within the party, hiding his ambition while acting as the leader's loyal right-hand man, eliminating rivals and replacing them with newcomers who had him to thank for their position. Saddam drew inspiration from other sources too. Early in his presidency he asked his half-brother, whom he had appointed head of intelligence, to collect books on Nazi Germany. The president reportedly wanted to learn how to organize society to achieve big goals.

Stories about Saddam's brutal regime leaked outside Iraq. Yet he also impressed outsiders by making positive changes. Life for the poorest Iraqis had improved, with better wages, free health care, and the literacy program Saddam had created as vice-president. The program was not voluntary, though—adults and children throughout the country were forced to attend reading classes. For the first time, all Iraqi children were attending school, but along with their new education came stern instruction in Baath ideology. Saddam founded youth groups to capture the hearts and minds of young people. "Some fathers have slipped away from us for various reasons," he said, "but the small boy is still in our hands."

A young member of "Saddam's Cubs" stands next to a portrait of the Iraqi president. Saddam Hussein set up summer camps where boys 13 to 16 trained with pistols and rifles, while also studying Islam and politics.

Youth group members swore oaths, wore uniforms, and held ranks that imitated the Baath Party structure. Saddam was especially keen that boys receive military training to mold "new men in the new society." Children's new loyalties to the youth group and the party were meant to replace old bonds. Children must be trained to resist their parents' "backwardness," Saddam explained. "You must encircle the adults through their sons … Teach students … to contradict their parents … You must place in every corner a son of the revolution, with a trustworthy eye and a firm mind who receives his instruction from the responsible center of the revolution."

Many Western countries, eager to secure an ally in the oil-rich region of the Persian Gulf, paid attention only to Saddam's positive actions. They found him modern and much more reasonable than the revolutionary government of Iran, Iraq's neighbor. Iran had made an enemy of the United States in 1979 when Islamic revolutionaries attacked the U.S. embassy, taking its employees hostage. With oil exports funding his regime, Saddam could see his boyhood dreams coming within reach. The powerful, united Arab state his uncle had talked about could be a reality. And Saddam would be the one to lead it.

Controlling the divided people of Iraq was not a simple task for Saddam. In the north, the Kurds stubbornly kept their own army and independence. In the south, opposition from Shia Muslims flared up from time to time. And Iran's new leader, the Ayatollah Khomeini, was not making it easier. In broadcasts he urged Iraq's Shia Muslims—who shared the same religion with

Iranians—to rebel against Saddam's regime. To Saddam's fury, Iran had even come to the aid of Iraq's rebellious Kurds. Border disputes had plagued Iraq and Iran for years, but now Khomeini presented himself as a holy voice uniting Muslims—in contrast to the worldly Arab state Saddam offered his citizens.

Saddam sized up Iran's strength. The country was still rocked by the revolution that had begun with the overthrow of its monarch, the shah. Its once-mighty forces were now reduced. Saddam's ambitions began to soar. The Iranians controlled the narrow waterway Iraq needed to enter the Persian Gulf. Removing them would leave Iraq free to dominate the area. This was also his chance to stamp out the source of Shia rebellion. It was time to strike, Saddam decided.

Saddam publicly tore up the peace accord previously signed by Iran and Iraq. From his bunker under the Presidential Palace, he ordered air and ground assaults against Iran. Iraq was equipped with Soviet weapons, whereas Iran was armed with American weapons left over from the days when the U.S. had supported the shah.

In the first years of the war, Iraqis at home did not suffer hardship, and life went on as usual. Saddam's control over Iraq's radio and television news allowed him to bolster his image through widespread propaganda. A 19-volume official biography celebrated his heroism. Saddam also ordered the filming of a six-hour idealized movie about his life, and to give the project flair he hired a director who had made two James Bond films. During the war, Saddam toured Iraq, visiting schools and religious houses. He was eager to look like a man of the people. On one typical visit, he arrived unannounced—but with a film crew—at a peasant's farm, dressed in a shepherd's sheepskin vest.

These goodwill tours came to a halt in 1982. On a visit to a mixed Sunni-Shia town, a gang of gunmen opened fire on the president. Saddam was trapped inside a building for two hours before the army arrived to rescue him. Shaken, he withdrew into his Presidential Palace and from then on rarely appeared in public. Bodyguards followed him everywhere, and tasters tested all his food for poison. Saddam recruited several doubles in order to confuse would-be assassins.

The war with Iran escalated, and the number of casualties mounted on each side. Against Iraq's superior weapons, Iran began to launch "human wave" assaults, sending huge numbers of men and boys, many unarmed, into the face of firing Iraqis. Saddam took his attacks to a terrible new level. Iranian soldiers were fired upon with artillery shells that let off heavy smoke that smelled like garlic. The soldiers' eyes burned and their skin itched, then turned red and blistered. They had been attacked with chemical weapons, and some had only days left to live. Inside Iraq, Saddam resolved to smash resistance from the Kurds once and for all. He ordered the same chemical weapons—mustard gas and nerve agents—to be unleashed against them.

The United Nations accused Saddam of breaking the 1925 Geneva Protocol that banned chemical weapons. Saddam denied the charge. But the evidence was impossible to hide: chemically burned victims had been sent to Europe for treatment.

The destructive war with Iran ended in a stalemate, with a ceasefire arranged by the UN. The damage done by the war was vast, and Iraq was left billions of dollars in debt. But Saddam claimed a victory. In Baghdad he erected a monument celebrating his triumph: two gigantic arms holding crossed swords.

Iraq had shown itself to be a mighty force in the Middle East, Saddam believed, and he had forged partnerships with powerful countries that had sided with him. Several nations even helped him build up his arsenal. The Soviet Union and France supplied Saddam with much of his weaponry. Germany sold him parts for advanced missiles. The Americans had advised Iraq on how to fight Iran, and convinced other Arab countries to sell Saddam weapons. The United States also gave Saddam equipment for weapons systems and shared secret information gathered from U.S. satellites.

SADDAM HUSSEIN: FACTS

Born: April 28, 1937 (official date)
Titles in power: President of Iraq, Chairman of the Revolutionary Command Council of the Baath Party, Field Marshal of Iraq's armies
Age upon coming to power: 42
Time in power: 24 years
Size of domain: Iraq, 437,072 sq. km (168,739 sq. miles)
Armed forces commanded: The fourth-largest army in the world in 1990, with 955,000 troops. Smaller air force and navy.
Number of victims: Human Rights Watch estimates at least 300,000 Iraqis.
Defining characteristics: cunning, suspicious, methodical
Legacy: Long-term impact of Saddam's terror campaigns and wars remains to be seen. Despite his extreme measures to impose unity, Iraq remains a divided society.

Saddam now commanded the most powerful armed force in the Persian Gulf region, and he would soon make it the fourth largest in the world. He had already ordered Iraqi scientists to begin secretly developing a nuclear bomb, as well as biological weapons that could inflict enormous damage by spreading disease. Only a nation possessing that kind of power, Saddam believed, could be truly strong.

Saddam's ultimate goal was to rule supreme in the Arab world. To do that, he needed money and oil, and he knew where to find plenty of both: Kuwait. Iraq's southern neighbor was demanding that Iraq repay the money it had borrowed during the war, and, to Saddam's fury, Kuwait refused to raise the price of oil—a strategy Saddam wanted to use to rebuild Iraq's ruined economy. Saddam decided to invade. But his gamble that other countries would stand by if he grabbed Kuwait did not pay off.

Saddam Hussein received a deadline from the United Nations: leave Kuwait by January 15, 1991. He ignored it. Now he faced an attack by a coalition army that included many of the countries that had formerly aided him. From the air, the coalition bombed Baghdad's electric power plants, communications centers, and factories.

News had spread of Saddam's chemical and biological weapons programs. U.S. troops had been vaccinated in case Iraq used biological weapons. But Saddam took seriously a warning from the U.S. government: if Iraq used any "weapon of mass destruction," they said, it would be dealt a blow from which it would take years to recover. Believing the Americans were threatening a nuclear attack, Saddam chose not to unleash his biological arsenal. His threats to the environment, however, were no bluff. Iraqi forces were ordered to start oil tank fires in Kuwait to hide their troop movements, and they later dumped thousands of barrels of oil into the Persian Gulf.

Saddam was facing a stronger enemy, but as his uncle Khairallah had taught him, he was not going to back down. His best hope was to split the alliance assembled against him. Saddam ordered that Scud missiles be fired against Israel, hoping to provoke a strike by that country against an Arab target. If Egypt or Syria were attacked, it might then break away from the U.S.-led coalition. Seeing the danger, the U.S. convinced Israel not to retaliate, and surrounded the country with its own missiles for protection.

Iraq's armed forces were no match for the superior weapons of the United States. Shortly after the coalition's ground invasion began in February 1991, Saddam announced that Iraq's troops were withdrawing from Kuwait. To his great relief, the U.S.-led forces stopped short of invading Iraq and capturing Baghdad. The goal had been the liberation of Kuwait, and the coalition risked losing international support if it pressed on any farther. Despite the overwhelming surrender of Iraqi soldiers to the coalition, Saddam made a victory speech: "You have won, Iraqis. Iraq is the one that is victorious."

As many in the coalition had hoped, Iraq's Kurds and Shia Muslims rose up against Saddam at the end of the year. They did not succeed, however, and Saddam was brutal in crushing them.

Columns of defeated Iraqi forces may have retreated back across the border at the end of the Persian Gulf

War, but around the world many people wondered: What about the biological, chemical, and nuclear weapons the coalition had feared? Did they exist? If so, where were they now? Would Saddam Hussein make more? The UN promised to lift its sanctions against Iraq on one condition: Saddam must prove that he had no weapons of mass destruction by letting inspectors into the country.

Iraqi commandos parade in Baghdad, passing under Saddam's victory arch of crossed swords built after the war with Iran. In 1998, Saddam made a rare public appearance to watch the display of this "volunteer army," recruited during the conflict with the UN over weapons inspections. After parading for six hours, 100,000 new troops pledged their allegiance to Saddam.

The Iraqi president agreed. But although UN inspectors were allowed into Iraq, they were kept from looking too closely at suspicious sites. Some members of the inspection team were expelled from the country for a time. While the inspectors did find and destroy chemical weapons, as well as large biological weapons facilities, they were not sure they had found them all. Throughout the 1990s, Saddam handed the UN a series of reports that he claimed fully disclosed his biological weapons program. But the UN considered them unbelievable.

Iraqis suffered greatly under the UN's economic sanctions. Prevented from selling its oil, Iraq's economy crumbled. High prices and low wages made Iraqis poorer; hunger and disease were everywhere. The UN offered an "oil for food" deal: Iraq could sell oil only if the money was used to buy food and medicine. But this did not solve Iraq's shortages altogether. According to one estimate, over a million Iraqis may have died because of the sanctions. To Saddam Hussein, however, that mattered less than buying time to build and protect his weapons arsenal.

Saddam continued to play cat and mouse with the UN. But he was playing a deadly game.

Saddam's relationship with his family had always been simple: in return for their complete obedience and loyalty, they could reap enormous profits. In the days when the U.S. supported Iraq, Saddam's wife was known for her million-dollar shopping sprees in New York. Saddam's elder son, Uday, had made himself extremely rich with his shady businesses, imports, and control of most of the country's media. During the war with Iran, while Saddam was asking Iraqis to donate their savings and jewelry to the nation, his son was enjoying his fleet of expensive sports cars and costly nightlife. Saddam tolerated his reckless son, hoping to groom Uday to take his place one day.

Yet this favored inner circle was plagued by jealousy. Saddam's relatives competed for signs of his approval, often profitable jobs involving arms and oil deals. They fought and intimidated one another. These troubles reached a climax in 1995.

Fearing that the ruthless Uday was out to kill them, two brothers who were married to daughters of Saddam fled the country with their wives and children. They took refuge in Jordan, where they were interviewed by the CIA, by Britain's intelligence service, and by the UN. In return for their inside information, the couples hoped they would be given a safe haven in the U.S. or Britain. One son-in-law offered shocking details about Iraq's hidden chemical weapons plants and the front companies that shielded purchases of weapons. He also revealed that Saddam had been close to testing an atomic bomb at the beginning of the Persian Gulf War.

Saddam was furious. Members of his Tikriti inner circle—including his own daughters—had slipped out of his control. He stopped eating and spoke to no one for a time. Then he took action. Through his security agents, he contacted the defectors in Jordan. Saddam then telephoned them himself. He promised to pardon them if they returned. His honor as head of the family had been wounded, he said, by the theft of his daughters. If they returned, all would be forgiven.

The fleeing couples had been given a cold welcome by the West, and it seemed they had taught Saddam a lesson. They decided to go back. But just across the border they were met by Uday and his guards. Uday ushered his sisters and their children into his car, and the two husbands were summoned to the Presidential Palace. There they were forced to sign divorce papers. Saddam tore the badges of rank off their uniforms and sent them to their father's home. They were gunned down by Saddam's guards shortly afterwards.

Saddam had begun to have doubts about Uday and turned his attention to his younger son, the quieter, more disciplined Qusay. But some close to Saddam secretly thought his chances of appointing an heir were slim. He could hold on to power by force for now, but passing the reins to one of his sons once he was gone, one insider said, was "wishful thinking."

On September 11, 2001, terrorists from a group known as al-Qaeda hijacked U.S. airplanes and flew them into the New York World Trade Center and the Pentagon in Washington, D.C., killing thousands of people. After the attacks, some members of the U.S. government suggested there might be a link between Saddam Hussein and al-Qaeda. Intelligence reports remained sketchy, however, and a connection between Saddam and the al-Qaeda terrorists was not discovered.

Saddam, as always, answered accusations with defiance. Although he denied any link to the terrorists, Saddam issued an "open letter" to the American people, denouncing the U.S. government. Soon after, he refused another UN request to allow weapons inspectors into Iraq. But Saddam's stalling tactics over inspections could not work forever. He was now under growing pressure from foreign powers hostile to his regime.

The United States and Britain announced that

Saddam was an international outlaw. He refused to give up his stash of weapons, they said, and he supported terrorists. In their view, this made him too dangerous to be allowed to stay in power. But international support for a war against Iraq was shakier this time than in 1991. Many countries were unconvinced that the use of force was justified, and UN members would not agree to authorize an invasion. Some questioned the U.S. government's motives for attacking Iraq. As tensions grew, people in the U.S., Britain, and other countries staged anti-war protests. Several Arab leaders asked Saddam to go into voluntary exile in order to avoid war. He refused.

In March 2003, Saddam Hussein received an ultimatum from U.S. president George W. Bush: leave Iraq with your sons within 48 hours or be attacked. Saddam remained, and the U.S.-led invasion of Iraq began. The Iraqi government and military collapsed within weeks, and Saddam lost control of the country. When Baghdad fell to the invaders in April, he could not be found. In July, Uday and Qusay were killed in a shootout with U.S. forces. Where their father was remained a mystery.

As in the past, Saddam had turned to his clan, going into hiding near his hometown. But the U.S. military obtained information from people close to Saddam. In December 2003, 600 U.S. soldiers descended on a farm south of Tikrit. They found Saddam, tattered and bearded, in a small underground hideout.

Iraq's new Governing Council shot questions at the captured dictator. What about the assassinations, the massacres, all the deaths he had caused? Saddam was "unrepentant and defiant," said the head of the Council. "He tried to justify his crimes … and said that he was a just but firm ruler. Our answer was that he was an unjust ruler because his crimes were responsible for the deaths of thousands of people."

MODERN DICTATORS, AGE-OLD STRATEGIES

Saddam Hussein is not the only tyrant of modern times. The years since Hitler and Stalin have seen the rise of many tyrants around the world. These modern dictators often use the same methods as past tyrants to seize and hold power.

François Duvalier ("Papa Doc"):
President of Haiti, 1957–71

A former doctor, François Duvalier had the support of the army when he was elected president of Haiti. Once in power, Duvalier recruited a secret police force, the Tontons Macoutes ("Bogeymen") to control the population. They combined violence with voodoo to frighten Haitians into obedience. Papa Doc encouraged the belief that his own voodoo practices gave him special powers. Upon Duvalier's death, his son, 19-year-old Jean-Claude Duvalier ("Baby Doc"), was proclaimed "president for life" and continued to terrorize the population. Baby Doc's human rights abuses led the United States to cut foreign aid to the country. Without support, and faced with revolts by his citizens, Duvalier was forced into exile in 1986.

Augusto Pinochet: President of Chile, 1973–90

Fear of what some believe is a greater evil has often led people to support a bad leader. And tyrants are opportunists who know how to take advantage of fear. In 1970, a socialist government led by Salvador Allende was elected in Chile. The new government did not win by a majority, and the country was torn between those for and against Allende. Western powers, especially the United States, were alarmed by the possibility of Communism taking hold in South America. The U.S. tried to weaken the new government by cutting off trade and financial aid, while lending support to the Chilean army. This set the stage for General Augusto Pinochet to lead the military in a violent takeover of the country. Under Pinochet's harsh regime, thousands of political opponents were arrested, tortured, and executed, although Pinochet denied such human rights abuses. After losing a popular vote, Pinochet stepped down as president in 1990, but he remained in command of the Chilean army until 1998.

Pol Pot: Leader of Cambodia, 1975–79

Pol Pot led his militant Communist party, the Khmer Rouge, in a takeover of Cambodia in 1975. His goal was to create an ideal farmers' society. Like Stalin before him, he transformed the country into a "peasant paradise" by force. Millions of people were herded out of the cities and onto collective farms. Anyone considered too "impure" to join the new society was eliminated: those who spoke a foreign language, the well educated, even those who wore glasses. Only by constant physical labor could people prove themselves loyal enough to be spared. Pol Pot's radical program killed over a million people—one out of every seven Cambodians. But this tyrant's ambitions led to his downfall. Cross-border attacks by the Khmer Rouge on Vietnam led that country to invade Cambodia and over-throw Pol Pot.

Idi Amin: President of Uganda, 1971–79

Uganda had recently become independent from Britain, and was split among many ethnic groups, when Amin, commander of the armed forces, deposed the president and seized power. The military strongman was too impatient to co-operate with his government ministers and began making all decisions himself. He expelled Asians from Uganda, targeted various tribes for persecution, and set the army above the law by empowering soldiers to arrest anyone they liked. Amin depended on the army for his power, and he purged from its ranks whole groups he suspected of disloyalty. Amin and his military supporters plundered the country, ordering the bank to print more currency when money ran out. Uganda, once rich in natural resources, became poor.

Idi Amin's crude methods could not keep him in power forever. The corrupt army was not able to defend the country when Tanzania, supported by rebel Ugandan troops, invaded. After urging his men to resist, Amin secretly fled Uganda.

Kim Jong Il: Leader of North Korea, 1994–present

For decades North Korea has been ruled by a one-man Communist dictatorship. After Kim Il Sung's death in 1994, his son Kim Jong Il took over.

Like his father, Kim Jong Il has flooded North Korea with propaganda designed to create a cult around himself as a supreme, flawless leader. Kim Il Sung was called "the perfect brain" and was said to know everything. After his death he was declared "president for eternity," and his son became "the central brain." For many years North Koreans have heard nothing but these official "truths," since both Kims have used the strategy of blocking foreigners and their ideas from the country, while shutting their citizens in.

Refugees who escaped into China and South Korea have described the total control Kim had over their lives: workers in North Korea live together in housing blocks where they can watch one another and receive daily instruction in party ideology. Many outsiders doubt the regime can survive; the country depends on foreign aid to feed the population, while resources are devoted to its army of one million men.

ENDING TYRANNY

What can we learn from the tyrants of the past? Since tyrants have used the same strategies over and over to get and keep power, we can recognize the signs of a tyrant today—and they do exist around the globe. There may not be a foolproof test to tell good leaders from bad, but a few key questions can help guide our thinking. Does a leader have the continued support of the majority of the people in his country, or does he use force to keep himself in power? Does he accept different opinions and criticism from political opponents? Is his authority limited by laws, or does he treat his own decisions as the law? What is the leader using his authority for—to improve the lives of his citizens or to increase his own power?

What defense is there against someone who abuses power? The stories of tyrants show that it is possible to resist them. Resistance, when it grows large enough, has even brought about their downfall—as it did for the Second Emperor of Qin, Nero, and Robespierre. In more recent times, widespread protests helped end dictatorships in countries such as Argentina and the Philippines. Personal acts of resistance against reigns of terror have also saved thousands of lives. In Nazi-occupied Europe, many people turned a blind eye to the deportation of Jews and other victims of the regime. But thousands of others did not: they hid their Jewish neighbors or helped them escape.

Tyrants count on the majority of people not caring about the wrongs done to a few. But when people refuse to look the other way, they put a major obstacle in a tyrant's path. That means standing up for others, even if what is happening to them doesn't directly affect you. It also means respecting everyone's right to voice an opinion—even when you strongly disagree. When people protect the rights of their opponents, they also guarantee their own freedom and safety. The French writer François Voltaire, who was twice imprisoned for his words, declared, "I may not agree with what you say, but I will defend to the death your right to say it."

Allowing different opinions puts a limit on how far a tyrant can take his program without running into opposition. The English historian Lord Acton wrote about power and its dangers. "Limitation is essential to authority," he said. No individual should be all-powerful. Decision making must be shared, and constitutions, laws, and courts are needed to keep too much power from gathering in one person's hands.

Knowledge is another defense. Modern technology has been abused by tyrants to flood a nation with their own propaganda. But the same tools of communication can be used against tyrants: it is harder to keep people ignorant of the truth in a world where information moves around freely through sources such as the Internet. That's why "watchdog" groups monitor the actions of governments around the world and publicize human rights abuses. No tyrant wants his secrets leaking to the outside.

Besides exposing his crimes, what can the countries of the world do about another nation's tyrant? After World War II, a group of countries formed the United

Nations to maintain international peace and to co-operate in solving world problems. The UN Security Council has the power to take action against any danger to world peace—it can cut off trade with an offending country or use force. But agreement among countries is needed first, especially among the UN's five permanent members: Britain, France, Russia, the United States, and China.

In the case of Saddam Hussein, UN members agreed that inspectors should check for weapons of mass destruction in Iraq. But when Saddam refused to co-operate fully, UN members were divided on what should happen next. The United States and Britain said the answer was to remove Saddam by force. Three of the strongest opponents to this plan were France, Germany, and Russia. In 2003, the United States and Britain decided to undertake the invasion anyway. But there is much debate about whether a superpower such as the U.S. was justified in using its military strength without UN approval.

The UN can confront a regime that threatens world security, but what it should do about a tyrant's crimes inside his own country is less clear. In theory, the UN should act only if these "domestic" problems threaten world peace. Yet most people agree it is wrong to do nothing about leaders who abuse their citizens' human rights. Countries can pressure a tyrant by denying him trade or financial aid. But sanctions can backfire when the people living under a tyrant suffer poverty because of a ruined economy. Still, such drastic measures have helped topple a dictator—as in the case of Haiti's Jean-Claude Duvalier.

Another possibility is to bring tyrants to justice in an international court. In the aftermath of wars in

Rwanda and the former Yugoslavia, the UN set up tribunals to bring political and military leaders to trial for war crimes and crimes against humanity. The International Criminal Court, formed in 2002, was a further step towards this goal.

Is there a way to stop tomorrow's tyrants before they get a foothold on power? Time and again, a tyrant's opportunity comes during a crisis, when people are desperate for change or afraid for the future. The greatest barrier to a tyrant's success has always been people who respect human rights and refuse to abandon their responsibility as citizens. Tyrants have plagued people throughout history. But we can use the lessons of the past to fight the tyrants of today and stop the tyrants of the future.

GLOSSARY

abdicate: to give up a position of authority, especially a monarch's throne

alchemists: scholars who, from ancient times to the Middle Ages, searched for ways to turn base metals into gold or for the secret to eternal life

Allies: the alliance of countries during World War II that included Great Britain, Canada, Australia, France, the Soviet Union, the United States, and others

atheist: a person who does not believe in God

boyars: Russian nobles (from the 900s to the 1600s) who owned land and owed military service to a prince or czar. A council of boyars advised the ruler.

caesar: title of the Roman emperors, taken from the name of Julius Caesar, a Roman general and dictator (100 BCE–44 BCE)

cold war: a power struggle between countries that does not involve actual combat, especially the conflict between the Western powers and the Soviet Union from the end of World War II to 1989

Communism: a movement that aimed to use revolution to create a society without social classes, in which all property would be owned in common

coup or **coup d'état:** a sudden, violent takeover of the government by a group

czar: title of the emperors of Russia, from the Latin *caesar*

delegate: a person chosen to represent others and act on their behalf, also called a deputy

dictator: a political leader with absolute authority. A dictator often seizes power in a *coup d'état*, but some are elected then throw off legal restraints once in office. The word originally described a Roman official given emergency powers for a limited time.

guillotine: a machine for executing people by beheading, with a blade that slides down between two posts. It was named after the French doctor who promoted it, Joseph Guillotin, and used by the government of the French Revolution.

gulag: forced-labor camp in the former Soviet Union where political opponents and anyone considered a threat by the Communist government could be sent

Mongols: people of the region of Asia lying between China and Russia

Reich: German word for *empire*

revolution: a total and often violent change in the government and society of a country

Soviet Union: (Union of Soviet Socialist Republics, or USSR) from 1922 to 1991, the name for Russia and 14 east European and north Asian republics under the control of the Communist Party. With the fall of Communism, the USSR collapsed in 1991 and the non-Russian republics asserted their independence.

Tatars: nomadic people of the Mongol region, conquered by the Mongol chief Genghis Khan. In the Middle Ages, Russians and Europeans used the name to describe all Mongol invaders.

United Nations: international organization of countries with the aim of maintaining world peace and security, formed after World War II

veto: the right to reject a proposed action

weapons of mass destruction: nuclear, chemical, and biological missiles and other weapons that are capable of causing widespread damage. Many countries are seeking to limit or ban them.

FURTHER READING

Qin Shi Huangdi
Dorothy Hinshaw Patent. *The Incredible Story of China's Buried Warriors.*
New York: Benchmark Books, 2000.

Nero
Elizabeth Powers. *Nero.* New York: Chelsea House, 1988.
Chris Scarre. *Chronicle of the Roman Emperors.* London: Thames and
Hudson, 1995.

Ivan the Terrible
Thomas G. Butson. *Ivan the Terrible.* New York: Chelsea House, 1987.

Robespierre
Susan Banfield. *The Rights of Man, the Reign of Terror: The Story of the
French Revolution.* New York: J.B. Lippincott, 1989.
S.L. Carson. *Maximilien Robespierre.* New York: Chelsea House, 1988.
Adrian Gilbert. *The French Revolution.* East Sussex, U.K.: Wayland, 1995.

Hitler
James Cross Giblin. *The Life and Death of Adolf Hitler.* New York:
Clarion, 2002.
Jennifer Keeley. *Life in the Hitler Youth.* San Diego: Lucent, 2000.

Stalin
David Downing. *Joseph Stalin.* Chicago: Heinemann Library, 2001.
Dorothy and Thomas Hoobler. *Joseph Stalin.* New York: Chelsea House,
1985.
Stewart Ross. *The USSR under Stalin.* New York: The Bookwright Press,
1991.

Saddam Hussein
Dale Anderson. *Saddam Hussein.* Minneapolis: Lerner Publications,
2004.
Charles J. Shields. *Saddam Hussein.* Philadelphia: Chelsea House, 2003.

MAIN SOURCES

Arthur Cotterell. *The First Emperor of China*. London: Penguin, 1981.

Sima Qian. *Records of the Grand Historian, Qin Dynasty*. Translated by Burton Watson. New York: Renditions–Columbia University Press, 1993.

Edward Champlin. *Nero*. Cambridge, MA: Harvard University Press, 2003.

Michael Grant. *Nero*. New York: Dorset Press, 1970.

Miriam T. Green. *Nero: The End of a Dynasty*. New Haven: Yale University Press, 1984.

Suetonius. *The Twelve Caesars*. Translated by Robert Graves. London: Penguin, 1957, 1979.

Tacitus. *The Annals of Imperial Rome*. Translated by Michael Grant. London: Penguin, 1996.

Correspondence between Prince A.M. Kurbsky and Tsar Ivan IV of Russia. Cambridge, U.K.: Cambridge University Press, 1955.

A.P. Pavlov. *Ivan the Terrible*. London: Longman, 2003.

Maureen Perrie. *The Image of Ivan the Terrible in Russian Folklore*. Cambridge, U.K.: Cambridge University Press, 1987.

Heinrich von Staden. *The Land and Government of Muscovy: A Sixteenth-century Account*. Translated by Thomas Esper. Stanford, CA: Stanford University Press, 1967.

John Hardman. *Robespierre*. London: Longman, 1999.

Colin Jones. *The Longman Companion to the French Revolution*. London: Longman, 1988.

David P. Jordan. *The Revolutionary Career of Maximilien Robespierre*. New York: Free Press, 1985.

J.M. Thompson. *Leaders of the French Revolution*. Oxford: Basil Blackwell, 1988.

Alan Bullock. *Hitler: A Study in Tyranny*. London: Harper & Row, 1962.

Alan Bullock. *Hitler and Stalin: Parallel Lives*. London: HarperCollins, 1991.

Adolf Hitler. *Mein Kampf*. Translated by Ralph Manheim. New York: Houghton Mifflin, 1971.

Ian Kershaw. *Hitler 1889–1936: Hubris*. London: Allen Lane/The Penguin Press, 1998.

Ian Kershaw. *Hitler 1936–1945: Nemesis*. London: Allen Lane/The Penguin Press, 2000.

Lawrence Rees. *The Nazis: A Warning from History*. New York: W.W. Norton, 1997.

Louis L. Snyder, ed. *Hitler's Third Reich: A Documentary History*. Chicago: Nelson-Hall, 1981.

Frederic Spotts. *Hitler and the Power of Aesthetics*. New York: Overlook Press, 2003.

Hugh Trevor-Roper. *Hitler's Table Talk 1941–1944: His Private Conversations*. London: Phoenix Press, 1953, 2000.

Sheila Fitzpatrick. *Everyday Stalinism. Ordinary Life in Extraordinary Times: Soviet Russia in the 1930s*. New York: Oxford University Press, 1999.

Martin McCauley. *Stalin and Stalinism*. 3rd ed. London: Pearson Education, 2003.

Chris Ward. *Stalin's Russia*. 2nd ed. New York: Oxford University Press, 1999.

Efraim Karsh and Inari Rautsi. *Saddam Hussein: A Political Biography*. New York: The Free Press, 1991.

Sandra Mackey. *The Reckoning: Iraq and the Legacy of Saddam Hussein*. New York: Norton, 2002.

David Schaffer, ed. *Iraq*. New York: Greenhaven Press, 2004.

Alan Axelrod and Charles Phillips. *Dictators and Tyrants: Absolute Rulers and Would-be Rulers in World History*. New York: Facts on File, 1995.

INDEX